Introduction to AWS Lambda and the Serverless Application Model

Gojko Adzic

Copyright

Title: Running Serverless
Subtitle: Introduction to AWS Lambda and the Serverless Application Model
Print ISBN: 978-0-9930881-5-5
Originally published: 1. July 2019.
Last updated: 15. January 2020.
Copyright (c): Neuri Consulting LLP 2019-2020
Author: Gojko Adzic
Copy-editor: Mary White
Illustrator: Nikola Korać

Published by:

Neuri Consulting LLP
25 Southampton Buildings
London WC2A1AL
United Kingdom

For all information about this book, including translation rights, send an email to:

contact@neuri.co.uk

Thanks to everyone who helped

Many people helped me write a better book, with great suggestions for additional resources and improvement ideas and by helping me fix factual errors. Thank you Alan Richardson, Aleksandar Simović, Alex Casalboni, Alvaro Garcia, Chris Haggstrom, Christian Pfisterer, Cyrille Martraire, Damjan Vujnović, Daniel Bryant, Daniel Zivkovic, Darryl Hughes, David Howell, Dejan Dimić, Gavin Manning, Ivica Kolenkaš, João Rosa, Lynn Langit, Marcus Hammarberg, Mashooq Badar, Michael Bolton, Michael Fagan, Mike Roberts, Paul Julius, Phil Hunt, Pieter Herroelen, Rich Vaughan, Rob Park, Shaolang Ai, Slobodan Stojanović, Vicenç García Altés.

Nikola Korać illustrated the book, and Mary White edited it. Thank you both for making the book much more enjoyable.

About the author

Gojko Adzic is a co-founder of MindMup, a mind-mapping collaboration tool which was one of the early adopters of AWS Lambda, and one of core contributors to Claudia.JS, a popular serverless deployment tool for JavaScript. He one of the 2019 AWS Serverless Heroes.

Gojko is a partner at Neuri Consulting LLP, winner of the 2016 European Software Testing Outstanding Achievement Award and the 2011 Most Influential Agile Testing Professional Award. Gojko's book Specification by Example won the Jolt Award for the best book of 2012, and his blog won the UK Agile Award for the best online publication in 2010. His other books include:

- Humans vs Computers
- Fifty Quick Ideas to Improve Your Tests
- Fifty Quick Ideas to Improve Your User Stories
- Impact Mapping
- Specification by Example
- Bridging the Communication Gap

To get in touch, write to gojko@neuri.co.uk or visit https://gojko.net.

Learn about updates

Serverless platforms are still rapidly evolving, and AWS is doing something important about AWS Lambda every few months. This makes it difficult to present long-term advice in a book. In fact, after I finished the first version of the book but before we could go to print, AWS released an update to the Node.js Lambda runtimes and an improvement to SAM that made the content of two chapters obsolete and required me to rewrite two more chapters from scratch. I decided to delay the release of the book so you can get up-to-date information rather than relying on old advice.

This version of the book captures the state of the platform as of January 2020, with AWS Lambda runtime for Nodejs 12.x and SAM 0.40.0.

I plan to keep the electronic version of the book up to date with new developments. If you want to learn about important changes in the future, and learn if something important has changed since I published this version of the book, check for updates at https://runningserverless.com. If you bought a paper or an electronic version of this book, then sign up for updates on the website and you'll get any future changes for free in an electronic form.

Contents

Introduction

This book will help you get started with AWS Lambda and the *Serverless Application Model* (SAM). Lambda is Amazon's engine for running event-driven functions, and SAM is an open-source toolkit that greatly simplifies configuring and deploying Lambda services. Together, they make it easy to create auto-scaling APIs and cloud services designed for *serverless* deployments. You will learn how to:

- Design applications that get the most out of serverless architectures
- Create auto-scaling web APIs
- Handle background tasks and messaging workflows
- Set up a deployment pipeline for effective team collaboration
- Test and troubleshoot code designed for AWS Lambda
- Inspect and monitor serverless applications

The contents of this book are based on my experiences with MindMup, a collaborative mind-mapping system that was one of the early adopters of AWS Lambda. MindMup moved to a serverless model from an application hosting service throughout 2016, in order to benefit from on-demand scaling. We reduced operational costs by about two-thirds while significantly increasing application capacity, speeding up development and reducing time to market for new features. The lessons from our migration ended up in one of the first scientific papers on the topic, and I was invited to present our experiences at conferences all over the world.

As I'm writing this in January 2020, with the hindsight of operating serverless for almost four years, it's easy to spot emerging architectural patterns and experiments that turned out to be good ideas, as well as those that led to dead ends. This book will help you go through that journey significantly faster, adopt good practices and avoid pitfalls.

This book is structured as a walk-through for building a practical application. We start from a simple static API and gradually grow it into an online image-resizing service, ready for millions of users, with all the supporting operational and infrastructural capabilities. The application closely resembles real-world systems that many of you will develop in your jobs. This will give you a good structure for your own work, and you will be able to almost copy parts to get a head start. As you discover how to create and deploy different parts of the application, you will also learn about key aspects of Lambda and related services, important tips, techniques and tools for running serverless.

The tutorial evolved from dozens of conference workshops and code camps. My colleagues and I have used the exercises from this book to teach hundreds of developers about serverless architectures, improving the examples through feedback into a great way to gradually introduce important concepts.

Why AWS SAM?

When we started moving MindMup to a serverless architecture, SAM was not yet available, so we had to write our own tooling for the same purpose. If we were to do the same thing now, SAM would be the obvious choice.

As a relative newcomer in the group of AWS Lambda deployment tools, SAM is not the most popular, most feature-rich or the easiest tool to use (at least when I wrote this). However, SAM hits a nice sweet spot of productivity and power and has a big advantage over the other tools, because it is backed by AWS. This means that it has strong commercial support, so it's a relatively safe bet for the future.

SAM users can benefit both from the freedom of an open-source tool and developer knowledge and internal access typical for closed commercial products. The tool is open source, with code on GitHub, making it easy to inspect and evaluate. The community around SAM is large enough for users to get help. At the same time, most of the contributors are AWS employees. The whole serverless ecosystem is still evolving quickly, and the fact that SAM developers have internal access to other AWS products and teams means that new platform features quickly find their way into SAM.

Adopting AWS SAM would be very easy for most organisations, because it is based on the de-facto standard for AWS deployment, CloudFormation. (I cover CloudFormation briefly in Chapter 3.) For companies already using CloudFormation, adopting AWS SAM just means slightly changing how they prepare Cloud-Formation templates, instead of implementing a completely new process or approving new tools. SAM greatly simplifies the boilerplate required to set up serverless infrastructures with CloudFormation, so it is much easier for beginners than using standard CloudFormation resources.

Intended audience

This book is a technical tutorial. It will be useful for two groups of developers and architects:

- People who have no previous experience working with serverless applications and are interested in learning about emerging cloud architectural patterns
- People who already work with Lambda using other deployment frameworks and want to learn about AWS SAM, the Serverless Application Model

You do not need any special prior knowledge about cloud services to understand the examples, but you will need to know how to at least read JavaScript code.

At the time when I wrote this, AWS Lambda would officially run software written for six runtimes: Open-JDK (for Java and related JVM languages), .NET Core (C#, Powershell and similar), Go, Ruby, Python and JavaScript. It is even possible to set up a custom runtime, so there are opensource implementations for some other popular languages.

The choice of the language for developing Lambda functions isn't hugely important, but to keep things consistent and make the book easy to read I had to select one of them. I've chosen JavaScript for the examples in the book, because it is the nearest to a common language for software developers in 2020. All the principles I present in the book apply equally to other languages, and I will point out important things that are different for a specific runtime. I will also provide fully working code for all the examples in some other languages, and you can download them from this book's website, https://runningserverless.com.

Reading the book

The first chapter is a quick introduction to the basic ideas of serverless applications and the benefits and challenges brought by this new way of running software. If you are completely new to AWS Lambda, read it as a teaser to see what operational changes you can expect. If you are already somewhat experienced with serverless deployments, you can skip the first chapter.

The second chapter explains how to set up SAM command line tools for developing and testing Lambda applications. Prepare your local development environment according to the instructions in the second chapter to try out the examples from this book while you are reading it. If you don't plan on trying the code immediately, skip this chapter.

The sections from Chapter 2 onwards are the tutorial for building a massively scalable application for the modern cloud. It's important that you read Chapters 2–12 in sequence. At the start, you'll learn about basic deployment tasks and how to effectively set up a team-working environment. As the application grows, you will learn more about higher-level concerns such as application architecture, choosing between AWS services, and making the most of serverless deployments. Important tips and tricks are spread throughout these chapters, so don't skip a section even if you already know the topic presented in the title.

The final chapter explains some common architectural and deployment solutions for typical tasks. Serverless is still a relatively new way of running applications, and it's way too early to talk about best practices, but this chapter will help you make a good start when designing systems to get the most out of AWS Lambda and associated services.

Source code

To help focus your attention on important parts and save some reading space, I will avoid most of the common boilerplate code in the examples. Anyone with working knowledge of JavaScript will be able to easily reconstruct the full application from this book, but the source code in the code listings is optimised for reading and understanding, not for copying and pasting.

You can download the full working source code for all the examples from https://runningserverless.com. Important source code listings show the related source code file name in the header. For example, the following listing can be found in the source code package, in lines 126 and 127 of the file titled template-with-dlq.yaml, inside the directory titled ch9 (Chapter 9).

—————————————— ch9/template-with-dlq.yaml ——————————————

```
26  NotifyAdmins:
27    Type: AWS::SNS::Topic
```

Command line examples

AWS command line tools often require a long list of parameters that exceeds the line length of a small screen or book page width. If there is not enough space for everything to fit on a single line, small continuation arrows will tell you that you should enter everything together. Here's an example:

```
sam deploy --template-file output.yaml --stack-name sam-test-1 --capabilities CAPABILITY_IAM
↳   --profile sam-test-profile --region us-east-1
```

To visually distinguish between inputs and results, the commands you need to type will not have line numbers next to them, but the results will have line numbers. For example, the next listing is how this book will show input commands:

```
aws sts get-caller-identity
```

The next listing shows the result of the previous command, with line numbers next to the printout:

```
1  $ aws sts get-caller-identity
2  {
3      "UserId": "111111111111",
4      "Account": "222222222222",
5      "Arn": "arn:aws:iam:1111111111:root"
6  }
```

Tips and notes

I will point out information you specifically need to pay attention to when running examples in a text box, such as the following one:

Source code

Don't copy and paste source code; get the whole package from https://runningserverless.com.

I will also use text boxes to explain key terms and important information to remember, especially ideas that might be counter-intuitive and therefore require special attention.

1. Serverless in five minutes

This chapter explains the financial and technical constraints of serverless deployments. You will learn when and why AWS Lambda is a good option for hosting software, and when you should use something else.

Serverless applications are, at the most basic technical level, software that runs in an environment where the hosting provider is fully responsible for infrastructural and operational tasks such as receiving network requests, scaling the computing infrastructure on demand, monitoring and recovery.

Instead of containers bundling application business logic with an operating system, network servers (such as web servers or message brokers) and business logic code, serverless applications only need to provide the code that should run when an event happens and configure the triggers in the execution environment to call that code.

In the Amazon Web Services cloud, the execution environment for serverless code is called *AWS Lambda*. It supports a wide array of potential triggers, including incoming HTTP requests, messages from a queue, customer emails, changes to database records, users authenticating, messages coming to web sockets, client device synchronisation and many more.

Because application developers do not package or distribute the server code to control a network socket in AWS Lambda, their applications are *serverless*. The buzzword 'serverless' is a horrible marketing term, and the internet is full of bad jokes about how there are still servers in a serverless environment. The right comparison to think about is WiFi. When you browse the internet using a 'wireless' connection in a coffee shop, your device talks to a router just a few feet away, and there is a wire coming out of that router and taking your packets to the internet. But you don't need to care about that wire or manage it actively. AWS Lambda is *serverless* in the same way WiFi is wireless. There are network servers, virtual and physical machines running in the background, but you don't really need to care about them any more.

Compared with running applications in a container cluster or managing virtual machines directly, serverless deployments have two big benefits:

- *Shorter time to market* for new features, leading to faster innovation and delivering value to customers sooner
- *Reduced operational costs* due to better resource utilisation

A study by the research company IDC[1] published in 2018 suggests that companies adopting serverless applications on average 'lowered five-year operating costs by 60% and were 89% faster at compute deployment'. This is roughly consistent with my experience. After MindMup moved from a host where we paid for reserved capacity to AWS Lambda, we reduced operational costs by almost two-thirds. Another popular case study is Yubl, presented by Yan Cui at various conferences over the last few years. Yubl reduced its operational costs by 95% by moving to Lambda. Both the MindMup and Yubl case studies are explained in more detail in the research paper *Serverless Computing: Economic and Architectural Impact*[2] which Robert Chatley and I co-authored.

In March 2018, Cloudability published the results of its *State of the Cloud*[3] research of AWS customers, suggesting that Lambda adoption increased by 667% in a year. This is not surprising, because the combination of reduced operational cost and faster path to customer value provides a very strong financial incentive for companies to adopt AWS Lambda and similar services. The key factor in both reduced costs and faster development is actually the same. It is the serverless pricing model.

---

[1] https://pages.awscloud.com/Gated_IDC_Generating_Value_Through_IT_Agility.html
[2] https://www.doc.ic.ac.uk/~rbc/papers/fse-serverless-17.pdf
[3] https://get.cloudability.com/ebook-state-of-cloud-2018.html

The serverless pricing model

Technically, AWS Lambda and similar systems are supercharged container management services. They provide standardised execution environments in order to activate applications very quickly, and algorithms to automatically scale containers according to the workload. Although running those services is technically challenging, this is just an incremental improvement on a decade-long journey towards application virtualisation. That's why technical architects, especially those who built and operated their own container clusters in large companies, sometimes complain how serverless is all just a marketing fad. What AWS did that was revolutionary with Lambda, and that other cloud providers are quickly copying, was the financial side of the story. The serverless pricing model is a lot more important than the technology for application developers.

When using AWS Lambda to run code, you pay for *actual usage*, not for *reserved capacity*. If the application isn't doing much, you don't pay for anything. If millions of users suddenly appear, Lambda will spin up containers to handle those requests, charge you for doing so, and then remove them as soon as they are no longer necessary. You never pay for idle infrastructure or when tasks are waiting on user requests.

Reserving minimum capacity

In December 2019 AWS enabled users to reserve minimum capacity for Lambda functions, ensuring that there is always a certain number of processes waiting on user requests. In the AWS jargon, this is called *Provisioned Concurrency*. With provisioned concurrency, you will also pay a fixed price for reserved instances, regardless of whether they are used or not. However, most applications won't need to use this feature, if you design them well.

Lambda pricing depends on two factors: the maximum memory allowed for a task, and the time it spent executing. As an illustration, assuming a configuration with 512 MB allowed memory, AWS charged the following fees for Lambda in the USA:

- $0.0000002 per request
- $0.000000833 for running 100ms with 512 MB working memory

Comparing reserved virtual machine pricing with paying for utilisation isn't straightforward, because they depend on different factors. Reserved capacity pricing usually depends on expected load, and utilisation pricing depends on the nature of tasks being executed. Here are two examples at various extremes.

For an infrequent task, say something that needs to run every five minutes for about 100 ms and needs 512 MB memory, Lambda pricing would roughly work out to slightly less than 1 US cent a month. Renting a similar hardware configuration from AWS Elastic Compute Cloud (EC2), assuming having a primary and a fail-over virtual machine in case of problems, would cost roughly 9 USD, three orders of magnitude more. Note that for Lambda, it's not necessary to reserve a backup system in case the primary one falls over; this is already provided by the platform and included in the price.

At the other extreme, a single Lambda function continuously receiving requests and never stopping over a month would cost roughly 27 USD. Just looking at basic hosting costs, reserving virtual machines seems cheaper. But this is only if we ignore all the operational services that are included with AWS Lambda and assume that a single virtual machine is enough to handle this sustained load. For something getting continuously hit over a long period of time, it's much more likely that it would run on a whole cluster of load-balanced machines, with several backup systems waiting in reserve. Working with virtual machines requires operations experts to carefully plan capacity, predict load and automate container cluster scaling to match expected demand. With Lambda, all that is included in the price, as well as recovery from errors, logging, monitoring and versioning.

The difference between billing for reserved capacity or for actual usage is also important for testing and staging environments. When companies pay for reserved capacity, copies of the production environment usually multiply the operational costs, even though they are idle most of the time. That is why staging and acceptance testing environments usually end up being slimmed-down versions of the real thing. With billing based on actual usage, environments don't cost anything if they are idle, so the economic benefits of maintaining separate slimmed versions disappear. For most organisations, testing environments with serverless architectures are effectively free.

For serverless applications, the provider controls the infrastructure, not the application developers. This means that developers can focus on things that make their application unique, the core business logic, and not waste time on operational or infrastructural tasks. When moving MindMup from a hosted environment based on virtual machines to AWS Lambda, we realised that we could drop a lot of source code that performed infrastructural tasks, and since late 2016 have not needed to write any serious infrastructural code at all. We didn't have to spend time building and integrating monitoring and scaling systems or worry about most operational issues. Lambda helped us go from a conceptual idea to working software in front of users significantly faster.

How request pricing affects deployment architecture

With serverless applications, developers write functions to coordinate and perform business features unique for their application, using platform services to manage state or communicate with users. In the case of AWS, the pricing for most of those services is also structured around utilisation, not reserved capacity. Amazon Simple Storage Service (S3), a scalable file system, charges users for transferred bytes in and out of the storage service. Amazon Simple Notification Service (SNS), a message topic system, charges for each sent message. The whole platform is designed so that how much you pay depends on how much you actually use the platform. Lambda is the universal glue that brings all those services together.

In his conference talk *Why the Fuss about Serverless*[4], Simon Wardley argued that serverless is effectively platform-as-a-service, or more precisely what platform-as-a-service was supposed to be before marketers took over the buzzword. No doubt history will repeat itself, and in a few years things that have nothing to do with these ideas will be sold as 'serverless'. But for now, here are what I consider the three critical aspects of a serverless application:

- Infrastructure providers are responsible for handling incoming network requests.
- Operational cost is based on actual utilisation, broken down by individual requests.

---

[4]https://www.youtube.com/watch?v=b7Nc_FJiosk

- Technical operations (deployment, scaling, security and monitoring) are included in the price.

These three factors make up an interesting set of deployment constraints. For example, with request-based pricing and no overhead to set up or operate environments, it costs exactly the same amount to send a million user requests to a single version of your application, or to two different versions, or to 50 different versions. *The number of requests matters, not the number of environments.*

Ever since the time of immortal mainframes, all popular deployment architectures had a significant overhead for creating a new execution environment. This is why staging and testing environments were commonly less powerful than the production one, and why developers and testers often fought each other for the control of a single integration test system in the company. Containers and virtual machines significantly reduced the time it takes to provision a new environment, but they did not change the mathematical formula for operational costs too much. Two equivalent copies of the production environment cost twice as much. That model created strong financial incentives to bundle features into applications that could be deployed together and reuse the same resources.

I recently worked with a consulting client where all the report generators were running on the same cluster, and a single slow report clogged the whole container it would run on, slowing down work for everything else that needed to happen. Separating out an environment for each report type would be economically silly, since most of them would sit idle most of the time. But when all reports end up in a single cluster, people need to carefully plan capacity and pay for reserved performance or suffer from delays during peak usage. With Lambda, capacity planning becomes Amazon's problem, and there are no specific benefits to bundling different workloads into a single cluster. Instead of aggregating tasks to save money in deployment, causing potential interference and performance bottlenecks, Lambda makes it economically viable to deploy each report type to an isolated infrastructure. Lambda price is proportional to the number of requests, not the number of workload clusters, so running a separate set for each report type costs exactly the same as when putting all report types in a single combined cluster. Even better, if those report generators have different memory needs, Lambda turns out to be cheaper. If everything is in the same cluster, the containers will need to reserve as much memory as the heaviest report process needs. With Lambda, processes with smaller memory needs can run in smaller containers, and cost significantly less.

With Lambda, you can create as many different versions of your whole infrastructure as you like without multiplying costs. Instead of developers and testers arguing over a single staging copy, create one for each team. Even better, create a full copy of your application for each developer or tester, with production-like capacity. It costs exactly the same as having a single version, because the price is based on the number of executed requests, not the number of environments.

How request pricing affects security

Request-based pricing also has a big impact on application security. Modern server-side applications usually run some kind of a gatekeeper process to control user requests and dispatch work. That process needs access to all the back-end services and all the databases and all the resources. It's possible to secure such processes tightly, but it's a big hassle. Most web servers usually run with database privileges that provide full access to everything. In case someone breaks into that process, the gates are completely open. With serverless deployments, security is much easier to control. Because there is no financial incentive to bundle tasks into a single application to reuse resources, each Lambda function can do a focused task and work under significantly restricted access privileges. It becomes easy to apply the principle of least privilege, allowing a task access only to resources and information required for its legitimate purpose. This helps with reducing the security blast radius in case of vulnerable third-party dependencies or hacks.

With pricing focused on requests, applications tend to be optimised for transient environments and dynamic infrastructure. The infrastructure provider can easily remove and replace underlying systems without interrupting application work. This has major implications for security patches. One day in August 2018, we got an email from a concerned client's IT administrator. He was asking about our plans to mitigate a security vulnerability in Intel processors, something that had hit the news the previous night. I pasted the security bulletin reference into Google to find out more details about the problem, and one of the first results was Amazon's announcement that Lambda was already patched. We didn't have to do anything. Because the service provider takes care of containers, it was able easily to drain traffic from old versions, send new requests to patched containers and just manage the whole thing for us.

How request pricing affects product decisions

Lambda pricing can also change how organisations release features. Do you have a customer with some very specific need, and you can implement a new feature for them in a few days, but it would take weeks more to build it up so it works for all your other customers? With Lambda, you can launch a new version for the specific customer as soon as the feature is ready, and keep everyone else on the old version until the feature is fully developed. Running two environments doesn't really cost any more than a single one.

Similarly, request-based pricing opens up new possibilities for testing features. Do you want to test how a change in a back-end process affects user conversion? Just create an experimental version of the application and send 10% of the traffic there. The number of users and requests is still the same, so running two versions costs the same as working with a single version. Running A/B split tests on the front end is easy, but organising that kind of work on back-end features was traditionally very expensive. Five years ago, only companies with massive computing resources, such as Google or Facebook, could run experiments on their back-end code continuously. With Lambda, that's now available to everyone, even a single-person team. It doesn't cost anything more than running a single version.

Another interesting aspect of the new pricing model is granular cost breakdown, down to every single request. In order for AWS to charge you correctly, it accounts for each request, and this information is also available to you as a customer. So it's now possible to understand the flow of capital through the application at a level of individual operations. You can calculate exactly how much money a single customer is costing you to serve, and decide whether it's worth keeping them around or not. You can calculate exactly how much money certain features cost to operate, and then decide whether they are worth enhancing or perhaps removing.

Important AWS Lambda technical constraints

Lambda is still a relatively new service, and it is evolving quickly. I often talk about serverless development at conferences, and it's been quite fun to review my slides about problems and constraints and have to remove things every few months. Things like start-up times and Payment Card Industry (PCI) data compliance were a serious limitation in 2017, but then got fixed. A common complaint against Lambda was that there was no service-level agreement guarantee for it, but in October 2018 AWS published an SLA for Lambda[5] as well. (It's currently 99.95%.)

By the time you read this the constraints might have changed slightly, but at the time when I wrote this there were four important technical limitations that you needed to consider when evaluating whether something should run in Lambda:

- No session affinity
- Non-deterministic latency
- Execution time limited to 15 minutes
- No direct control over processing power

No session affinity

Because the hosting provider controls scaling, you generally don't get to decide about starting up or shutting down instances. Lambda will decide whether it needs to create new virtual machines to handle requests, and when to reuse an old machine and when to drop it. It might send two subsequent requests coming from the same user to the same container or to two different containers.

Purely on Lambda, there is no way to control request routing or somehow ensure that requests from the same source arrive in sequence to the same destination. You can achieve sequences and routing control with some other services such as AWS Kinesis, but Lambda can still decide at any point to throw away a virtual machine and start a new one.

This limitation, coupled with the naming around functions, sometimes causes misunderstanding about the Lambda execution model. Lambda functions are not stateless, at least not in the pure functional programming sense where nothing is kept between two executions. Each instance still has a container with its local memory space, and if Lambda decides to reuse a virtual machine, two requests might still be able to share state in memory. Virtual machines also have access to a temporary local disk space, so it's possible to store information between requests on disk. But there are no guarantees about preserving state across requests, and application developers have no control over the routing.

It's best not to count on any in-memory state between two different requests in Lambda. When designing for Lambda functions, don't design for stateless execution, design for a share-nothing architecture. You can

---

[5]https://aws.amazon.com/lambda/sla/

still cache or pre-calculate things that do not depend on a particular user, but user sessions and state have to be somewhere else. There are several alternatives for session data. I will explain these options in Chapter 7 and Chapter 8. In the final chapter, I also explain some typical ways of sharing state or configuration between Lambda functions.

Non-deterministic latency

Lambda is optimised for maximising throughput, not for minimising latency. It prioritises handling a large number of requests so that none of them have to wait too long over handling a single request in a minimum amount of time. This means that some requests will need to wait for a new Lambda instance to start, and some will not. The latency of processing a single request isn't really deterministic.

A *cold start*, in the serverless jargon, is when an incoming request needs to wait for a new Lambda instance for processing. Early on, Lambda cold starts were a few seconds long on average. Many blog posts appeared on the topic of keeping some Lambdas in reserve, *warm*, to avoid cold starts. Since the early days, Lambda start-up times have improved significantly, so for most cases you can probably ignore that old advice. AWS does not publish any official information about cold starts, but my empirical tests suggest that with JavaScript or Python, the cold start is less than half a second. With Java and C#, it still may take a bit longer depending on the application size, which is another reason why I prefer using lightweight environments for Lambda. For a more detailed (but still unofficial) analysis of cold start times, check out Mikhail Shilkov's analysis of Cold Starts[6].

In late 2019 (after the first version of this book was published), AWS significantly improved start-up times for Lambda functions connected to a virtual private clouds (VPC). For applications that cannot avoid a lengthy initialisation, they also enabled users to reserve minimum capacity, reducing the problem of cold starts.

Limited execution time

Another major technical constraint is the total allowed execution time. Currently, a Lambda function is allowed to run for three seconds by default, and you can configure it to allow up to 15 minutes. If a task does not complete in the allowed time, Lambda will kill the virtual machine and send back a timeout error.

The 15-minute limit is a hard constraint now, so unless you have a very special relationship with AWS, you can't ask for a longer allowance. Long running tasks need to be split and executed in different batches or executed on a different service. AWS offers some alternative services such as Fargate that cost more and start more slowly but can run for a longer period of time.

In many cases, designing the application with Lambda in mind will help you work around the execution time constraint. For example, instead of using Lambda to start a remote task and then wait for it to complete, split that into two Lambdas. The first just sends a request to a remote service, and then the incoming response kicks off a different Lambda. You can use AWS Step Functions to coordinate workflows that last up to one year, and invoke Lambda functions when required. Don't pay for waiting.

---

[6]https://mikhail.io/serverless/coldstarts/aws/

No direct control over processing power

The last major technical constraint of Lambda is around choosing processors. Today, it is usual for container execution environments to offer a whole buffet of processor combinations, including GPUs, various CPU speeds or numbers of cores and instances optimised for certain types of tasks. However, with Lambda you don't get to choose any of that. The only container choice you can make is the amount of memory, from 128 MB to about 3 GB. Lambda is not good for tasks that require GPUs.

The memory configuration has an indirect impact on processing power. Lambda allocates CPU power in proportion to memory, so that at 1792 MB a function has access to one full virtual CPU[7]. With Node.js, all tasks run through a single core anyway, so with JavaScript you won't get any further processing speed improvements if you ask for more than 1.75 GB. With Java or other languages that can take advantage of multiple cores, asking for the maximum allowed memory might give you faster responses and lower cost for CPU-intensive tasks.

Lambda pricing depends on two factors: basic price for memory allocation and time spent executing. The fact that higher memory also leads to more CPU power can result in counter-intuitive cost structures. Allocating more memory raises the basic price, but more CPU power can lead to significantly shorter execution, reducing the price.

Because there are no direct controls for processing power, the best way to optimise costs and performance is to explore various parameter combinations. Luckily, AWS Lambda makes it easy to change these settings quickly and operate multiple versions in parallel cheaply. For tasks that become expensive or slow, I strongly suggest trying out several memory allocation options to find a sweet spot between price and performance. Alex Casalboni's opensource project AWS Lambda Power Tuning[8] can help you visualize the performance for various configurations of your Lambda functions.

When to use Lambda

Lambda is great for use cases where throughput is critical and the tasks parallelise nicely. Typical web requests for dynamic content, involving access to a back-end database or some user data manipulation, usually fall into this category. Automatic email replies or chatbots are also a nice example. Any single request taking a few hundred milliseconds more than average won't be noticeable to typical users, and Lambda will ensure that everyone gets served relatively quickly regardless of traffic spikes.

Longer on-demand computational tasks that can execute in less than 15 minutes, or could be split into independent segments take less than 15 minutes, are also a good use case for Lambda. In cases such as that, a few hundred milliseconds required for Lambda functions to start won't make an important difference to processing time. Some nice examples of tasks that fall into this category are file format conversions, generating previews or thumbnails, and running periodic reports.

Tasks that need high availability and good operational infrastructure, but do not need to guarantee latency, are also a great use case for AWS Lambda. This includes payment notifications from external systems, for

---

[7]https://docs.aws.amazon.com/lambda/latest/dg/resource-model.html
[8]https://github.com/alexcasalboni/aws-lambda-power-tuning

example PayPal or Stripe. These notifications must be handled reliably and relatively quickly, they might have unpredictable traffic patterns, and yet it's not critically important if they are finished in a second or two seconds.

Lambda is currently not suitable for tasks that require guaranteed latency, such as in high-frequency trading systems or near-real-time control systems. If a task must be handled in under 10 or 20 ms, it's much better to create a reserved cluster and have services directly connected to a message broker.

Another category where Lambda isn't suitable now is tasks that could potentially run for longer than 15 minutes. One notable example is video transcoding for large files. Connecting to a socket and consuming a continuous data feed is also not a good use case for Lambda, due to the time limit.

The third category where I would not use Lambda now is tasks that require a huge amount of processing power and coordination, for example video rendering. Tasks like that are better suited to a reserved infrastructure with a lot of CPUs (or even GPUs).

Lastly, tasks that require no on-demand computation, such as serving static web files, are a poor use case for Lambda. In theory, it's possible to use Lambda as a web server and send images and CSS files to clients, but this is a waste of money. It is much cheaper and faster to use a specialised product for that, for example a content delivery network.

A nice aspect of Lambda is that it works well with all the other services in AWS, so it's possible to incrementally adopt a serverless approach for certain tasks and use more specialised AWS products for tasks where Lambda does not fit nicely. You can read about some typical ways to combine Lambda with other services in Chapter 13.

Starting from Chapter 3, we'll build a service that combines the first two categories of tasks from this section: web processing with background file conversions. But first, we'll need to set up some tools to make it easier to develop and test serverless applications.

Interesting experiments

- Analyse the application you are currently working on and identify several individual tasks that the code is performing.
- Evaluate the latency and throughput needs of each task, along with parallelisation, duration and session constraints. Identify tasks that would be suited for running as Lambda functions.
- List the minimal security requirements for selected tasks and compare them with the access rights that they have in your current application.
- Try estimating the cost of running those tasks in AWS Lambda.

Part I

Basic development tasks

2. Set up tools for local development

This chapter explains how to install and configure AWS SAM command line tools and prerequisites.

The AWS Serverless Application Model (SAM) is a set of products that simplify developing, testing and deploying applications using AWS Lambda. One part of SAM runs on developer machines and build servers, helping to prepare for deployment. Another aspect of SAM runs in AWS data centres during the deployment process. As is unfortunately the case with much AWS software, these products have overlapping names. Nobody outside Amazon really cares too much about the distinction, so informally they all get called SAM. Although it is possible to use different SAM products separately, in most cases they work together, so a clean separation between them isn't especially important. In this chapter, we'll set up the first part of SAM, which runs on developer machines.[1] In the next chapter we will take a deeper look at the part of SAM that runs remotely in AWS.

SAM development tools help with building and packaging projects for deployment to AWS, debugging and simulating a Lambda environment, retrieving logs and generating sample events for testing. We'll set up command line tools, so you can use them with any editor, integrated development environment or build system. Various AWS toolkits for popular editors and development environments also include these tools, making it possible to test, simulate and debug Lambda functions directly from a visual interface. The AWS Cloud9[2] cloud-based integrated development environment also supports SAM tools.

Setting up prerequisites

AWS SAM CLI depends on a set of underlying tools which I'll explain below but whose full setup instructions are out of the scope of this book. That kind of information is easy to find online once you know what to look for, and it is likely to be updated more frequently directly on the individual tool websites. If you experience any problems with installing the tools below or want to use an alternative way of managing the packages, check out the *AWS SAM Developer Guide*[3] online.

The SAM command line tools are actually a set of Python scripts, so you will need the Python runtime installed on your machine. You can use Python 2 version 2.7 or later, or Python 3 version 3.6 or later. Most Linux and MacOS machines already have some version of Python installed. If you are unsure about this, check whether Python is installed and which version you have by running the following command:

```
python --version
```

If this command prints an error or you are using an outdated version, you will need to upgrade Python. In case you need to upgrade or install Python, get the one-click installer from https://www.python.org.

In addition to the Python runtime, you will also need to have the pip package management tool. Most Python installations already have one. To check whether it is installed on your machine, run the following command:

```
pip --version
```

---

[1]This product was previously called 'SAM-local', and today AWS documentation calls it the SAM Command Line Interface (SAM CLI). The main command line tool, which you'll be installing and executing, is just called sam.

[2]https://aws.amazon.com/cloud9/

[3]https://docs.aws.amazon.com/serverless-application-model/index.html

If this command prints an error, pip is missing on your system, so install it using the instructions from https://pip.pypa.io.

The final prerequisite is the basic AWS command line tools package. Most developers that access AWS in any way usually have those tools already installed. To check whether your system already has these tools, run the following command:

```
aws --version
```

If the command prints an error, you can download the tools by running the following command:

```
pip install awscli
```

Alternatively, get a ZIP or a binary installer for your operating system from the AWS CLI documentation site[4].

Installing on MacOS

In order for Python to work on MacOS, you will also need to set up basic development command line tools. You can install them by running the following command:

```
xcode-select --install
```

If you installed Python using brew, make sure it's version 2.7 or later. Older versions will not work well with SAM.

SAM tools use Docker, a container management system, to simulate the Lambda execution environment for local testing and debugging. You don't need to install the full Docker service; the free (community) Docker Desktop tools are enough for all development tasks, including working with all the examples from this book. If you do not have Docker Desktop tools already installed, get the one-click installer for your operating system directly at the Docker website[5]. You will not need Docker to actually run the code in production.

Installing JavaScript tools

In this book, we'll be using JavaScript with Node.js for developing Lambda functions. (You do not need Node.js to work with SAM in a different language, but you will need the appropriate tools for that language.) To try examples from the book directly, you'll need Node.js 12 or later installed. To check whether Node.js is installed on your machine, run the following command:

```
node --version
```

Get the Node.js installer for your operating system from https://nodejs.org/ if this command prints an error.

---

[4]https://docs.aws.amazon.com/cli/
[5]https://www.docker.com/products/docker-desktop

The latest Node.js version currently supported by Lambda is 12. I suggest getting Node 12 even if you have a more recent installation. You can manage multiple versions of Node.js on the same system using the Node Version Manager[6].

Installing the SAM command line tools

There are several ways of installing the SAM command line tools. If you use Homebrew or Linuxbrew package management tools, you can install AWS SAM CLI using the following commands:

```
brew tap aws/tap
brew install aws-sam-cli
```

Alternatively, use the pip package manager to download sam. Run the following command:

```
pip install aws-sam-cli
```

To check whether the installation worked, run the following command:

```
sam --version
```

If you get a response similar to the next listing, the software is ready:

```
1  $ sam --version
2  SAM CLI, version 0.40.0
```

If you get an error or the command is not found, you may need to restart the shell so that the new environment variables take effect. If that fails as well, check out the prerequisites again and then see the alternative installation instructions in the AWS SAM developer guide[7] online.

Running in an isolated environment

For any Python developers reading this, SAM works perfectly fine in a virtual environment. My preferred way of installing tools such as SAM is to create an environment for each project, so the tools and libraries are completely separate. If you want to use an isolated installation and avoid changing system packages, just set up a new virtualenv environment before running pip.

---

[6]https://github.com/creationix/nvm
[7]https://docs.aws.amazon.com/serverless-application-model/index.html

Configuring access credentials

AWS SAM CLI reuses the credentials configuration from AWS command line tools. If you already have credentials set up for AWS CLI, skip this section.

To deploy software to the AWS cloud, you will need an access key ID and a secret key ID associated with your user account. If you do not have these already, here is how you can generate a set of keys:

1. Sign in to the AWS Web Console at https://aws.amazon.com/.
2. Select the Identity and Access Management (IAM) service.
3. In the left-hand IAM menu, select *Users*.
4. Click on the *Add User* button.
5. On the next screen, enter a name for the user account then, in the 'Select AWS access type' section, select *Programmatic access* (Figure 2.1).
6. Click the *Next* button to assign permissions, then select *Attach existing policies directly*.
7. In the list of policies, find the PowerUserAccess and IAMFullAccess policies and tick the check boxes next to them.
8. You can skip the remaining wizard steps. The final page will show the access key ID and show a link to reveal the secret key (Figure 2.2). Reveal the secret key and copy both keys somewhere.

Figure 2.1: *Create a user with programmatic access rights for SAM and AWS command line tools.*

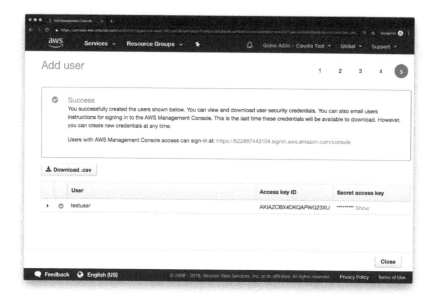

Figure 2.2: *In the final step, reveal and copy the access key and secret key.*

Once you have the access keys, run the following command to save the keys to your local machine:

```
aws configure
```

The AWS utility will ask you about the keys, so paste what you copied in the previous step. You will also likely be asked to enter a default region and a default output format.

For the default output format, enter json, or just press Enter to keep it unset.

For the region, use us-east-1 or check whether your IT administrators have a preference. Because AWS adds new regions and services frequently, for a full list of available options it is best to check out the *AWS regions and endpoints*[8] documentation page.

AWS regions

AWS has data centres all over the world. The region setting tells the command line tools which data centre to use. Region selection is useful to ensure that user data is hosted in a specific country for compliance reasons, or to speed up data transfers by using the closest available access point. The original AWS data centre in North Virginia is us-east-1. Generally, new services launch first in that region, so it is a safe setting for experiments.

Check that your credentials are correctly configured by running the following command line:

---

[8]https://docs.aws.amazon.com/general/latest/gr/rande.html

```
aws sts get-caller-identity
```

If this command prints a result similar to the next listing, everything works correctly:

```
$ aws sts get-caller-identity
{
    "UserId": "111111111111",
    "Account": "222222222222",
    "Arn": "arn:aws:iam:1111111111:root"
}
```

If you get an error, check out the section *Configuring the AWS CLI*[9] from the AWS CLI user guide for troubleshooting information.

Running with restricted user accounts

For trying out examples in the book, it's easiest to use access keys related to a user with full access to all AWS resources. If you created access keys as suggested in the previous section, those keys will have full access to all your resources, so you can skip this section.

If you would like to set up an account with restricted privileges, the user account will need the following policies:

- arn:aws:iam::aws:policy/AWSLambdaFullAccess
- arn:aws:iam::aws:policy/AmazonAPIGatewayAdministrator
- arn:aws:iam::aws:policy/IAMFullAccess

In addition, the user account will need access to CloudFormation. There are no standard AWS policies for this, so you will need to create a new policy and assign it to the user account. The JSON template below provides full access to all CloudFormation resources:

```
{
  "Version": "2012-10-17",
  "Statement": [
    {
      "Effect": "Allow",
      "Action": "cloudformation:*",
      "Resource": "*"
    }
  ]
}
```

---

[9]https://docs.aws.amazon.com/cli/latest/userguide/cli-chap-configure.html

Some companies restrict user accounts for developers, in which case you may need to ask your administrator to assign the policies mentioned.

If full access to IAM and CloudFormation is a problem, ask the administrator to create a separate subaccount for you in your AWS account organisation (the administrator can do so from the AWS Organisations console). Each sub-account has completely isolated resources, so granting full access on a subaccount does not assign any privileges to important corporate resources.

Using a profile

AWS command line tools can store multiple combinations of access keys on the same system. This is a convenient way to use separate access credentials for different projects or to reduce the chance of mistakes by restricting everyday usage to read-only access. A key combination is called a *profile*.

If your IT administrator creates a subaccount for experiments, different from your main AWS account, you will most likely want to record the keys into a separate profile in order to easily switch between access combinations. If your account is managed by a company and the IT security department does not want to give you the required access to try out SAM, you can register a personal account with AWS and set it up as a separate profile.

You can set up a profile by adding the --profile option to the command for configuring access keys, followed by a profile name. For example, the following command will help you create a profile called samdevelop:

```
aws configure --profile samdevelop
```

To use a specific profile, add the --profile argument to all the AWS and SAM commands. For example, execute the following command to test whether the profile samdevelop is set up correctly:

```
aws sts get-caller-identity --profile samdevelop
```

To keep things simple, I will omit the profile setting from the rest of the book. If you would like to use a separate profile, remember to add it to all the command line examples starting with aws or sam.

Now that the tools are ready, let's put them to good use by creating a Lambda function.

Interesting experiments

- Try locating the nearest AWS region to you and note down its identifier.
- Try creating a new profile for development, using a new set of access keys.
- Change the default output format for AWS command line tools to text or table and see how it impacts the commands used to verify that a profile is valid.

3. Create a web service

This chapter introduces the basic workflow for serverless deployments. You'll learn how to manage infrastructure with the AWS Serverless Application Model (SAM) and CloudFormation, and how to use API Gateway to send HTTP requests to Lambda functions.

SAM command line tools can generate sample projects and events, so you can get started easily. Let's dive right in and create a sample web service backed by a Lambda function. To create a simple SAM project in a new subdirectory, run the following command:

```
sam init --runtime nodejs12.x --name app --app-template hello-world
```

You should get a quick confirmation about the initialisation of a new project:

```
1  $ sam init --runtime nodejs12.x --name app --app-template hello-world
2
3  Cloning app templates from https://github.com/awslabs/aws-sam-cli-app-templates.git
4
5  ----------------------
6  Generating application:
7  ----------------------
8  Name: app
9  Runtime: nodejs12.x
10 Dependency Manager: npm
11 Application Template: hello-world
12 Output Directory: .
```

If this command printed an error instead, go back to Chapter 2 for information on how to set up SAM command line tools and the prerequisites.

The --runtime argument tells SAM which programming language we'll use to write the Lambda function, or more precisely which execution environment it is intended to run in. The --runtime argument is important just for generating the sample project. You will learn later how to add more functions to the same project, and you can even mix functions executing in different languages.

To speed up scaling and operations, Lambda has pre-packaged execution environments, called *runtimes*, for many popular languages. The nodejs12.x runtime tells Lambda to run our function under Node.js 12, an execution engine for JavaScript. SAM can also create example projects in other languages. For example, use java8 for a Java function. Check out the AWS Lambda runtimes[1] page for a complete list.

The --name argument tells SAM how to call the application, or more precisely the name for the subdirectory where to store the application files. In the previous example case we used app, so SAM will create a new subdirectory called app and copy the sample files there. Here are the key ones:

- hello-world is a directory containing the JavaScript (Node) source code for our Lambda function.
- hello-world/package.json is the standard Node.js package manifest, describing dependencies required by the function.
- hello-world/app.js is the actual service request handler.
- template.yaml describes the operational infrastructure required by the function.

The --app-template argument tells SAM which template to apply when initialising the application. You can see the list of standard templates in the aws-sam-cli-app-templates[2] project on GitHub. SAM can also use your templates, which might be useful for teams that often create similar Lambda functions. For example,

---

[1]https://docs.amazon.com/lambda/latest/dg/lambda-runtimes.html
[2]https://github.com/awslabs/aws-sam-cli-app-templates

you could create a template for message queue handling, and then quickly apply it when creating a new payment processor that connects to your payments queue. Companies can also use templates to standardise project directory layouts. To specify your own template location, use the --location parameter and point to a GIT repository or a local directory.

Infrastructure as code

For deploying applications, SAM uses CloudFormation, an AWS service for managing infrastructure as code. This means that CloudFormation converts a source file describing an application infrastructure (called *template*) into a set of running, configured cloud resources (called *stack*). Instead of individually configuring different resources such as file storage, databases and queues with CloudFormation, you just need to declare the required resources in a textual file. The template.yaml file in our project directory is a CloudFormation template.

We can use CloudFormation to create a whole stack of resources from the template in a single command. It is also smart enough to detect differences between a template and a deployed stack, making it easy to update infrastructure resources in the future. We can modify the template file, and CloudFormation will reconfigure or delete only the resources that actually need to change. If a resource update fails for whatever reason, CloudFormation will reset all the other resources to the previous configuration, managing a whole set of infrastructural components as a single unit. This makes it easy and safe for a whole team of developers to add, remove or reconfigure infrastructural services supporting an application. It also becomes trivially simple to know which version of infrastructure is compatible with which version of code. This supports infrastructure traceability and reproducible installations. It's not a coincidence that the template file is in the same directory as the function source; they should be committed to a version control system together.

Another benefit of CloudFormation is that you can share templates with other teams, or even publish them online, so that others can set up your application with a single click.

CloudFormation template formats

CloudFormation supports JSON and YAML template formats. In this book, we'll use YAML because it is easier to read in print. One downside of YAML is that whitespace is important and getting the right indentation might be a bit fiddly. If you want more control over the structure of your templates, feel free to use JSON instead. YAML is actually a superset of JSON, so you can also embed JSON into YAML for sections where you want to make structure clear and avoid problems with whitespace.

Open the template.yaml file in a text editor and you'll see the infrastructural description for a basic web service. (I've removed comments in the following code listings, for simplicity.)

The first line tells CloudFormation which syntax version to use:

```
AWSTemplateFormatVersion: '2010-09-09'
```

This is an optional setting, so you can omit it in your templates, but it is a good practice to explicitly specify the syntax version in case it changes in the future. Note, though, that the current version is 2010-09-09, which means it hasn't really changed since September 2010. If you don't specify the version, CloudFormation will use the latest available.

The second line in the example file tells CloudFormation to transform a template before executing it:

```
2   Transform: AWS::Serverless-2016-10-31
```

Generally speaking, with CloudFormation this is an optional setting. The part of SAM that runs in AWS data centres actually works as a CloudFormation transformation, so pretty much all your SAM applications will list a transformation at this point.

In this case and for the rest of the book, we'll use the AWS::Serverless-2016-10-31 transformation[3]. Don't be distracted by the date in the transform name; SAM gets updated frequently, and this is just a syntax version label. The transform setting activates SAM features and resources, allowing us to use compact descriptions for many building blocks commonly used in serverless applications. For example, this transformation allows us to use the AWS::Serverless::Function resource in CloudFormation as a replacement for AWS::Lambda::Function. It provides sensible defaults for security roles and logging, and makes it easy to connect Lambda to other AWS services. Similarly, we can use AWS::Serverless::Api to set up API Gateway resources more easily than with AWS::ApiGateway::RestApi, and AWS::Serverless::SimpleTable to configure DynamoDB database tables easily.

Using serverless resources without SAM command line tools

In order to use SAM CloudFormation transformation, you don't need any software locally installed. You can just add the Transform header into your CloudFormation templates and deploy it using standard CloudFormation tools. The transformation physically executes inside AWS CloudFormation, as part of the normal deployment pipeline, not on development machines or a continuous integration server uploading the template to AWS.

After the transformation comes the template description:

```
3   Description: >
4     app
5
6     Sample SAM Template for app
```

The Description section contains a free-form explanation of the template. This section is useful if you want to publish the template or give it to another team, but isn't necessary. You can safely skip it when creating templates for small experiments.

After the description, the example SAM template contains global application settings. This is a SAM-specific extension to CloudFormation and enables us to reduce the overall template file size by listing common set-

---

[3]https://docs.aws.amazon.com/AWSCloudFormation/latest/UserGuide/transform-aws-serverless.html

Multi-line text in YAML

YAML files usually contain text values on the same line as the corresponding key. You can use the right angle bracket (>) or a pipe (|) to signal that what follows is multi-line text, indented one level. The difference is that > removes line breaks from the result, and | preserves line breaks.

tings in a single place instead of repeating them for each Lambda function. The example template contains just a single function, so adding global values doesn't make a lot of difference, but this section is useful for more complex applications. The sample template usually contains a global Timeout setting, the number of seconds the function is allowed to run in Lambda:

```
Globals:
  Function:
    Timeout: 3
```

Next comes the Resources section, listing the services or resources for CloudFormation to configure:

```
Resources:
  HelloWorldFunction:
    Type: AWS::Serverless::Function
    Properties:
      CodeUri: hello-world/
      Handler: app.lambdaHandler
      Runtime: nodejs12.x
      Events:
        HelloWorld:
          Type: Api
          Properties:
            Path: /hello
            Method: get
```

This is where things become really interesting. With CloudFormation, each resource starts with its own block. The first line specifying a resource is the *logical ID* of the resource. In the sample template, HelloWorldFunction is a logical ID of a Lambda function. The logical ID is an internal name that CloudFormation uses to refer to a resource in a single template. It is effectively a variable name, and you can use it to refer to a resource when connecting it with other resources within the same template.

CloudFormation will create the actual ('physical') function name using a randomised string based on the logical ID. This makes it possible to create several instances of the same infrastructure in a single AWS account (for example, for development, testing and production), without causing any resource conflicts.

Each resource needs to specify a Type property which tells CloudFormation what to create. For the HelloWorldFunction, the type is AWS::Serverless::Function. This is another SAM extension to CloudFormation, making it easy to set up Lambda functions. You will use almost always use this type when creating Lambda functions with SAM.

Do not set resource names

CloudFormation allows you to specify names for many resource types, including functions, using the Name property. Unless there is a very specific reason why you need this, avoid setting physical names. Letting CloudFormation set random names makes it easy to create several stacks based on the same template and avoid resource naming conflicts.

Following the type, a template usually lists configuration properties for a resource, depending on its type. The following three properties are required for a Lambda function:

- CodeUri points to the source code package for the function. This is usually a local directory with the source code, relative to the SAM template file.
- Runtime is the execution engine for the function.
- Handler is the main execution entry point.

Specifying Lambda handlers

The Lambda handler is the main function responsible for processing incoming requests. The format of this setting depends on the runtime type. For Node.js, the format is module.function, where module is the file name (without the .js extension). The previous example points at app.lambdaHandler, meaning the function lambdaHandler in the app.js file.

Serverless functions can have some other properties, which I'll introduce in the following chapters. For now, only the Events property is important. Lambda functions usually run in response to some external events. The Events property configures a set of triggers for the function. Structurally, this property resembles the main Resources section. Each event has a logical ID followed by Type and Properties, which are type-specific event configuration attributes.

The example template sets up an HTTPS service, so it declares an Api event type. This represents API Gateway, an AWS service that can accept client HTTP requests. We will use a browser to send HTTPS requests to API Gateway, and the gateway will pass requests to our Lambda function. For Api event types, it's important to specify the HTTP method and request path. The example template sets up a Lambda call when clients request the /hello path, using the GET method.

This template involves another AWS service, which is not explicitly listed. It is called Identity and Access Management (IAM). IAM lets us configure access policies for AWS resources. If we just create a Lambda function without configuring IAM, no other AWS service will be allowed to invoke it. To actually make the function do something useful, we need to let IAM know who is allowed to send requests to it. SAM makes this easy, because it will automatically set up the correct security privileges from event definitions. Because we have a single event configured to invoke a Lambda function from API Gateway, SAM will tell IAM to allow this connection automatically (Figure 3.1).

The last few lines of the template specify outputs, normally listing key information required for the users of a template or for clients connecting to this application. You will see logical identifiers used as variables in

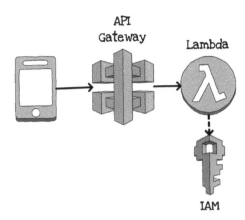

Figure 3.1: *Basic infrastructure set up by the sample template: API Gateway will be able to receive HTTP requests from clients and call a Lambda function to handle the requests. An IAM policy tells Lambda who is allowed to invoke it.*

the output values. CloudFormation will replace those values with actual physical resource identifiers once it creates the stack.

```
Outputs:
  HelloWorldApi:
    Description: "API Gateway endpoint URL for Prod stage for Hello World function"
    Value: !Sub "https://${ServerlessRestApi}.execute-api.${AWS::Region}.amazonaws.com/Prod/hello/"
  HelloWorldFunction:
    Description: "Hello World Lambda Function ARN"
    Value: !GetAtt HelloWorldFunction.Arn
  HelloWorldFunctionIamRole:
    Description: "Implicit IAM Role created for Hello World function"
    Value: !GetAtt HelloWorldFunctionRole.Arn
```

The first web service I created with Lambda, in early 2016 before SAM was available, had less than 20 lines of code but required about 200 lines of configuration scripts to set everything up. With SAM, we can achieve the same thing in just 10-15 lines of CloudFormation templates. Not bad!

Serverless functions or Lambda functions

CloudFormation has another resource for Lambda functions, AWS::Lambda::Function. SAM extends it with AWS::Serverless::Function. The benefit of using the SAM version is that it automatically creates IAM policies and event triggers. If you want to have more direct control over IAM and trigger invocation, use the lower-level resource instead, but you will then need to create security policies yourself.

The Lambda programming model

In the sample template, the combination of `CodeUri`, `Handler` and `Runtime` means that the Lambda environment will try to execute the code using Node.js version 12, by calling the function called `lambdaHandler` inside `app.js` in the `hello-world` directory. Find that file and inspect it, so you can see how Lambda responds to HTTP requests. It will look similar to the following code:

─────────────────── basic-template/hello-world/app.js ───────────────────

```
1   let response;
2   exports.lambdaHandler = async (event, context) => {
3     try {
4       response = {
5         'statusCode': 200,
6         'body': JSON.stringify({
7           message: 'hello world',
8         })
9       }
10    } catch (err) {
11      console.log(err);
12      return err;
13    }
14    return response;
15  };
```

Note that SAM generates a source file with lots of comments, and I've removed them from the previous listing in order to focus on important aspects of the function. Also, different versions of SAM contain different starter templates, so the file might not look exactly like in this book, but the interfaces are the same. You can find a version used in this book in the source code package from https://runningserverless.com.

The Lambda function is *asynchronous* in JavaScript, meaning that it has to either be marked as async (line 2 in the previous listing) or return a `Promise`. For other runtimes, that is not so important. (Previous versions of Lambda runtimes for Node.js also supported callbacks, but this is now discouraged and we will not cover that approach in this book.)

All Lambda functions have two arguments:

- `event` represents the data sent by the client invoking the function. In this case, it will contain the information about the HTTP request.
- `context` contains useful information about the runtime environment, such as the allowed execution time or logging setup.

In case of HTTP requests, the Lambda function needs to respond with an object containing the status code and the body of the HTTP response. API Gateway will assume that the response is a JSON object (hence the JSON.stringify call on line 7). You can modify this response to send back text or even HTML, and we will do that in Chapter 6.

Lambda interfaces in strongly typed languages

In strongly typed languages, such as Java, you can set up functions with specific request types and interfaces. In languages without strong typing, such as Python or JavaScript, these objects are mostly native key-value dictionaries or hash maps.

Deploying SAM applications

CloudFormation is amazingly powerful. It can deploy and configure almost any resource type available in the Amazon cloud, safely upgrading and downgrading entire networks of services. However, in order to achieve such flexibility, CloudFormation also needs to be very generic. It does not know about the structure of JavaScript, Python or Java projects, and it does not understand how to interact with programming language packages or dependency managers. In order to create a Lambda function, CloudFormation expects a fully self-contained ZIP archive. That archive needs to contain all the required files for the Lambda function, including source or compiled code, third-party dependencies and native binary packages. And it needs to be somewhere on Amazon S3, where CloudFormation can read it.

The complicated deployment process is the reason why there are so many packaging tools for Lambda functions, including the AWS SAM command line tools. SAM understands the typical project layouts for various programming languages and knows how to interact with platform package managers.

In the example project, the CodeUri parameter for a Lambda function points to a local directory with source code files. This is quite usual for teamwork and storing in a version control system, and you will use this approach in almost all projects. But we cannot send that template directly to AWS. In general, turning a SAM application on your disk into resources running in AWS requires three steps (Figure 3.2):

1. Build: create a clean copy of all Lambda functions, remove test and development resources, and download third-party dependencies.
2. Package: bundle each function into a self-contained ZIP archive and upload to S3, and produce a copy of the source application template that points to remote resources instead of local directories.
3. Deploy: upload the packaged template to CloudFormation, and execute the changes to create a running infrastructure.

Step 1: Build

Most modern software programming languages make it easy to reference third-party libraries and packages. For example, Node.js comes with NPM, a package manager that installs libraries listed in the package.json

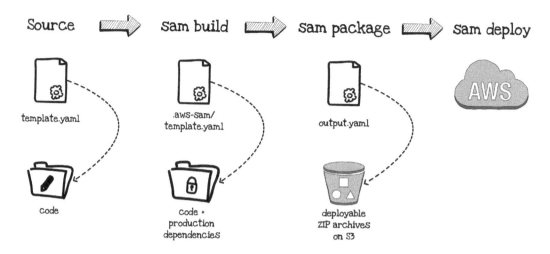

Figure 3.2: *Deploying with SAM: 'sam build' creates a local self-contained copy, the 'sam package' function packages to S3, and 'sam deploy' creates a stack using CloudFormation.*

project manifest. Python works with pip. Java has maven. In order for Lambda functions to start as quickly as possible, we need to install and bundle dependencies before uploading to AWS. CloudFormation doesn't know how to do that. However, the SAM command line tools know how to install and bundle dependencies for many common package managers. For compiled languages, such as Java and Go, SAM knows how to turn source files into executable code.

To prepare function source for uploading to AWS, execute the following command in the main project directory (app), the one that contains the CloudFormation template (template.yaml):

```
sam build
```

You should see a report that SAM built the HelloWorldFunction using npm:

```
1   $ sam build
2   2020-02-08 23:23:14 Found credentials in shared credentials file: ~/.aws/credentials
3   2020-02-08 23:23:14 Building resource 'HelloWorldFunction'
4   2020-02-08 23:23:14 'nodejs' runtime has not been validated!
5   2020-02-08 23:23:14 Running NodejsNpmBuilder:NpmPack
6   2020-02-08 23:23:15 Running NodejsNpmBuilder:CopySource
7   2020-02-08 23:23:15 Running NodejsNpmBuilder:NpmInstall
8
9   Build Succeeded
10
11  Built Artifacts  : .aws-sam/build
12  Built Template   : .aws-sam/build/template.yaml
```

The sam build command copies project source files into a temporary subdirectory and runs the required packager to install all production dependencies for functions. It knows how to ignore test code and resources and avoid bundling development dependencies. This means that you can safely install development tools in your source directory; SAM will ignore them when building the functions.

If your build process needs to compile binary executables, pass the --use-container option to sam build. This will execute the build process inside a Docker container matching the Lambda runtime. For JavaScript this is normally not needed. On the other hand, many Python libraries try to compile native dependencies, and building inside a Lambda-like container is very useful for those cases.

SAM creates a temporary directory for build artefacts, by default using a subdirectory inside your project called .aws-sam. You can make it write the build results to a different location by using the --build-dir option. Check out the SAM Build documentation[4] for more information on this and other options.

Building packages for other languages

At the time when I wrote this, in January 2020, SAM command line tools supported building JavaScript, Python, Ruby, Java and Go projects. This feature was under active development then, so it is likely that support for other languages will have been implemented by the time you start reading this book.

If your chosen packaging system is not yet supported, you will have to somehow bundle dependencies and remove development tools before uploading the code to CloudFormation. In this case, you can skip the sam build step.

Step 2: Package

The next step is to bundle all the files required by each function into separate ZIP archives and upload the results to S3. In order to do that, we will first need an S3 bucket to host our function packages. In the continuous delivery jargon, this will be our binary artefact storage. Think of a nice bucket name then create a new S3 bucket using the following command line (replace BUCKET-NAME with your chosen name):

```
aws s3 mb s3://BUCKET-NAME
```

For example, to create a bucket called sam-project-deployment, run the following command:

```
aws s3 mb s3://sam-project-deployment
```

S3 was one of the first services AWS launched, way back in March 2006, when they weren't yet thinking too much about conquering the world. As a result, all bucket names are unique, globally, across accounts. You will not be able to use sam-project-deployment, because that bucket belongs to me. Think of a nice name for your deployment bucket and remember to use it instead of my bucket name when deploying your examples.

You can safely reuse the same binary artefact storage for all your projects, so you do not need to create a separate bucket for each deployment.

---

[4]https://docs.aws.amazon.com/serverless-application-model/latest/developerguide/sam-cli-command-reference-sam-build.html

Deploying to a specific AWS region

AWS command line tools, including SAM CLI, allow users to select a specific data centre with the --region option. If you want to create resources in a specific region, add --region followed by the AWS data centre identifier to the command line. For example, to create a bucket in London, use the following command:

```
aws s3 mb s3://bucket --region eu-west-2
```

If you use a specific region for deployment, remember to add the --region argument to all the commands starting with aws or sam in this book.

SAM has a convenient shortcut to zip up and upload function packages to S3. Just run the following command in the directory containing the CloudFormation template (template.yaml), and remember to use your bucket name:

```
sam package --s3-bucket sam-project-deployment --output-template-file output.yaml
```

This command will produce another CloudFormation template, saving it into the file called output.yaml, as requested in the command parameter --output-template-file. Look at the file contents, and you will see that it is almost identical to the original template.yaml. The difference will be in the CodeUri property of the Lambda function, which points to a remote location on S3 in the output template. That's where SAM uploaded your Lambda function code. The function definition should look similar to the following block:

```
10  Resources:
11    HelloWorldFunction:
12      Properties:
13        CodeUri: s3://sam-project-deployment/ecf4c7e8862642e4942f766736df99f0
```

When you run sam package, it will print out a deployment command. This command is not correct for the first deployment, because it is missing the security permissions required to set up IAM roles. Do not copy what sam package printed, but instead execute the command from the next section.

SAM or CloudFormation packaging

CloudFormation also has a package command, and in fact sam package is just a wrapper around it. The benefit of using the sam command is that you do not have to specify an input template file. This is especially useful if you want to use sam build for installing dependencies, because SAM then uses the built copy instead of the original source. If you are not using SAM to build projects, there is no big difference between the two packaging processes.

Step 3: Deploy

We now have a single CloudFormation template (output.yaml) which describes the entire infrastructure and links to a packaged version of the function code. To create a running instance of our application, we'll need to create a new CloudFormation stack based on this template. To do that, run the following command in the directory that contains the packaged template (output.yaml):

```
sam deploy --template-file output.yaml --stack-name sam-test-1 --capabilities CAPABILITY_IAM
```

This command has three arguments:

- --template-file is the template to deploy. We want to use the result of the package command here, hence output.yaml.
- --stack-name is a name for the target stack. If a stack with the specified name does not yet exist in your AWS account, CloudFormation will create it. If you use the same name the next time you deploy, CloudFormation will update the existing resources instead of creating new ones.
- --capabilities CAPABILITY_IAM allows CloudFormation to create IAM policies. SAM needs this to let API Gateway call Lambda functions. Note that these are not security capabilities of the Lambda function, but instead the privileges required by the deployment process.

In a few moments, you will see that SAM has started deploying your project:

```
1  $ sam deploy --template-file output.yaml --stack-name sam-test-1 --capabilities CAPABILITY_IAM
2
3  Waiting for changeset to be created..
4  Waiting for stack create/update to complete
5  Successfully created/updated stack - sam-test-1
```

If you see permission errors instead of a successful result, make sure that you have configured access credentials for the command line tools correctly, and that your AWS access user has permissions to modify AWS resources. You can find instructions on configuring access credentials in Chapter 2.

SAM or CloudFormation deployment

The sam deploy command is more than just an alias for aws cloudformation deploy. It can store build parameters for your project in a temporary directory for easier reuse, and even run a guided deployment where it will interactively prompt you for the necessary inputs. Run sam deploy --guided for an interactive guided mode.

Inspecting a stack

Our first SAM function is live and ready to receive traffic. We just need to find out where SAM actually put it. For that, we'll need to look at the stack outputs. The easiest way to inspect a stack is with the AWS Web Console. Here is how to find information about a stack:

1. Sign in to the AWS Web Console, at https://aws.amazon.com/.
2. Find the CloudFormation service.
3. Make sure that the region selector in the top-right corner is showing the region where you deployed the stack. For us-east-1, the region name is US East (N. Virginia).
4. In the list of stacks, click on sam-test-1 (or whatever you called the stack).
5. The console will show information about your stack, divided into several tabs.

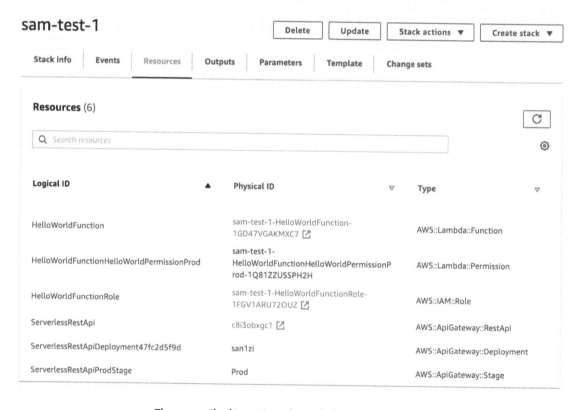

Figure 3.3: *CloudFormation web console shows stack resources*

The *Resources* tab (Figure 3.3) contains a list of all the AWS resources CloudFormation created for a stack. In the *Type* column, you should see a Lambda function, API Gateway, an IAM role and some additional API Gateway resources. Note that the Type value in the same row as the HelloWorldFunction says AWS::Lambda::Function, although the template requested AWS::Serverless::Function. This is because SAM resources (AWS::Serverless) are just higher-level templates that get transformed into lower-level AWS resources. Those transformations are activated by the header line Transform: AWS::Serverless-2016-10-31.

The *Outputs* tab contains a list of stack results, requested in the Outputs section of the template. These outputs are useful for combining stacks by using the results of one template as inputs into another. I often use stack outputs as a convenient way to point out important resources.

Switch to the *Outputs* tab and click on the link next to the HelloWorldApi output value. This is the web address where API Gateway expects our requests. Open it in a browser, and you should see the Lambda function in action (Figure 3.4).

Figure 3.4: *Lambda responds with Hello World!*

Inspecting a stack from the command line

The web console is a nice interface for discovering new information, but if you know what you are looking for, it's much faster to find it using the AWS command line tools. Instead of pointing and clicking, run the following command line:

```
aws cloudformation describe-stacks --stack-name sam-test-1
```

You will see all the information about the stack directly in your console. To avoid reading through irrelevant information, you can also reduce the output by providing a --query parameter. For example, list just the outputs using --query Stacks[].Outputs:

```
1   $ aws cloudformation describe-stacks --stack-name sam-test-1 --query Stacks[].Outputs
2   [
3     {
4       "OutputKey": "HelloWorldFunctionIamRole",
5       "OutputValue": "arn:aws:iam::111122223333:role/sam-test-1-HelloWorldFunctionRole-EGC56VNRV60R",
6       "Description": "Implicit IAM Role created for Hello World function"
7     },
8     {
9       "OutputKey": "HelloWorldApi",
10      "OutputValue": "https://ijdyjfw2a3.execute-api.us-east-1.amazonaws.com/Prod/hello/",
11      "Description": "API Gateway endpoint URL for Prod stage for Hello World function"
12    },
13    {
14      "OutputKey": "HelloWorldFunction",
15      "OutputValue":
     ↪    "arn:aws:lambda:us-east-1:111122223333:function:sam-test-1-HelloWorldFunction-QL5VEY42DZ2C",
16      "Description": "Hello World Lambda Function ARN"
17    }
18  ]
```

JSON output is nice if you need to pass this into another tool, but for humans you can also add --output text or --output table to format the results more nicely.

The --query value Stacks[].Outputs means 'find the Outputs key in all elements of the Stacks array and ignore anything else'. AWS command line tools use the JMESPath query syntax, which makes it possible to do complex searching, filtering and transformations of the results. For example, we can pull out just the output value for a key matching HelloWorldAPI, in order to use it as a shell environment variable or pass it to another command. Here is a command that does that:

```
aws cloudformation describe-stacks --stack-name sam-test-1 --output text --query
↪  'Stacks[].Outputs[?OutputKey==`HelloWorldApi`][OutputValue]'
```

Backticks and quotes in Windows and Linux command lines

To run the previous command on Windows, you may need to remove the single quotes around the query parameter. On Linux and MacOS, you will most likely need to keep single quotes around the value to prevent the shell from interpreting HelloWorldApi as a command because of the back-ticks.

I'll keep things simple in this book and avoid complex JMESPath queries, but remember that the JMESPath query syntax is quite a powerful option for automating reports on the command line. Check out http://jmespath.org for more information.

To see the list of resources in a stack from the command line, run the following command:

```
aws cloudformation describe-stack-resources --stack-name sam-test-1
```

Now that you know how to create a Lambda function, it's time to look at some common development tasks.

Interesting experiments

- Try deploying the stack again using the same name.
- Try creating a new stack, using a different name, from the same output template (you don't need to build and package again, just deploy under a new name).
- Try changing the response message in the Lambda function source and update only one of the deployed stacks, then compare the results.
- Try updating a stack with a broken CloudFormation output template, for example by modifying the CodeUri for the function to point to an invalid URL directly in output.yaml before deploying. Observe the deployment in the AWS Web Console and see how CloudFormation restores it to the last known working state.
- Run aws cloudformation help to see the full list of available CloudFormation tools, then experiment with some of them. For example, try deleting one of the deployed stacks.

.

4. Development and troubleshooting

This chapter explains the basic monitoring and logging features of AWS Lambda to help with troubleshooting. You will also learn how to simulate AWS services locally to speed up development work.

In the previous chapter we deployed a 'hello world' service that doesn't do much, but it comes with the full operational support required for serving millions of concurrent users. That's one of the best things about AWS Lambda. A five-minute hack is usually insecure, does not scale well and generally is not ready for production usage. Monitoring, scaling, fault tolerance, load balancing and centralised logging come out of the box with Lambda. Serverless is like those toys that have batteries included, instantly ready for playing with. (Note, though, that application developers still need to set up the correct security policies, which I cover in Chapter 7.)

Check out the operational status of your Lambda function by finding it in the AWS Web Console:

1. Open https://aws.amazon.com in a browser, and sign in if necessary.
2. Be sure to select the region where you deployed the stack, in the top-right corner. For example, if you deployed to us-east-1, the right region to select is 'US East (N. Virginia)'.
3. Select *CloudFormation* from the service list.
4. Select a stack (we created sam-test-1 in the previous chapter).
5. Open the *Resources* tab and click on the link in the *Physical ID* column corresponding to HelloWorld-Function (the one that has AWS::Lambda::Function in the Type column).

You should see the main screen of the Lambda console for your function, listing the function configuration (Figure 4.1). You can use this screen to set function parameters or even edit and replace the source code. Editing function properties directly in the web console might be useful for quick experimentation. I strongly suggest using SAM and CloudFormation to manage functions that you actually care about, in order to perform reliable and reproducible deployments.

The Lambda web console importantly shows the services authorised to call a function, below and left of the function box. In Figure 4.1 you can see that in our stack so far, only API Gateway can invoke the function. SAM automatically set up the authorisation because the application template contains API events. The web page also shows authorised outgoing connections from a function, below and right of the function box. Although our application template does not request any specific outgoing connections, SAM allowed the function to call one other service, Amazon CloudWatch Logs, as you can see in Figure 4.1. Because Lambda functions run on auto-scaling infrastructure, it's not possible to connect to containers and inspect them directly. System logs are the most important way of observing function behaviour. SAM assumes that in most cases developers want to capture function system logs, and sets up the CloudWatch Logs service for that purpose. Reliable centralised logging for a highly distributed system is a huge technical challenge, but with Lambda that comes with the basic setup and is included in the price.

Open the *Monitoring* tab (centre left), and you'll see a bunch of useful operational information about your function. For example, you should see the number of previous invocations, how long they took to execute, and the number of failed invocations (Figure 4.2).

Retrieving execution logs

The *Monitoring* tab also has a quick link to inspect CloudWatch logs. Click the *View logs in Cloudwatch* button (shown centre right in Figure 4.2), and you'll see the CloudWatch log group for your function.

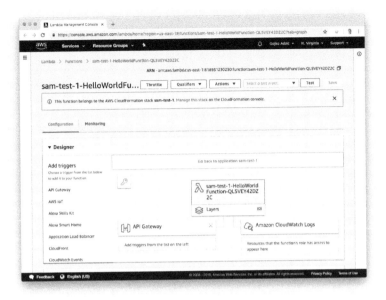

Figure 4.1: *Lambda console shows the configuration of a function, along with authorised incoming and outgoing connections.*

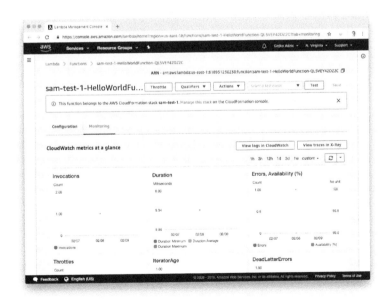

Figure 4.2: *The Monitoring tab shows operational statistics, such as invocation and error counts.*

CloudWatch groups logs into two levels of hierarchy: log groups and log streams. *Log groups* correspond to a logical service. AWS Lambda creates a log group for each function. A single log group can have multiple *log streams*, which typically correspond to a single running process. Lambda creates a log stream for each container instance (each *cold start*). If Lambda reuses the container for subsequent requests, the logs will appear in the same stream. If it creates a new container, the logs will appear in a new stream (Figure 4.3).

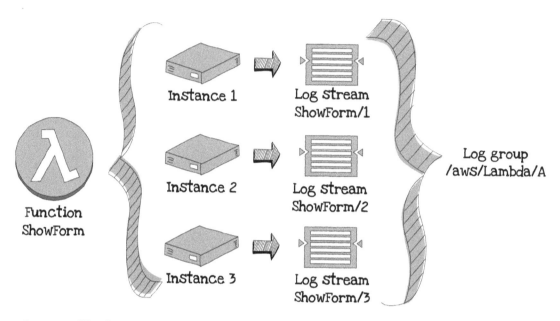

Figure 4.3: *All logs from a single Lambda function go to the same log group. Entries from a single running Lambda process go to the same log stream.*

Click the most recent log stream link, and you'll see the details about the function execution, including the total time it took to run, how much memory it used and the ID of the request (Figure 4.4). This information is incredibly useful if you start getting errors from an API. You can see if requests are timing out (so you need to increase the allowed time) or if they are hitting the memory limit (in which case you might want to increase the container size).

Lambda logs are not instantaneous

It might take a few seconds between a function logging a message and that information appearing in CloudWatch, so don't panic if your logs do not immediately appear. That's the price to pay for working with a highly distributed deployment.

Figure 4.4: *CloudWatch logs show details of a single Lambda function call.*

Retrieving logs from the command line

Navigating through web pages just to see the logs isn't really good for a quick development flow. The SAM command line tools have a convenient shortcut that lets us get the logs quickly. Poke the function web page again so it generates a recent log entry, and then run the following command:

```
sam logs -n HelloWorldFunction --stack-name sam-test-1
```

Here is what the arguments mean:

- -n (or --name) is the name of the function whose logs you want to retrieve
- --stack-name is the name of the stack that owns the function

You can either provide the full physical name of the function, in which case the stack name is not important, or provide the logical name of the function and the stack name. The first way of invoking sam logs is useful for retrieving logs from functions created outside CloudFormation, but the second way of invoking is often more convenient for functions created using SAM.

You'll see the log output directly in your command window:

```
1  $ sam logs -n HelloWorldFunction --stack-name sam-test-1
2  2020/02/10/[$LATEST]85c744cede7f405997aff8198ce0604e 2020-02-10T13:01:44.718000 END RequestId:
   ↪   6b2b4dc3-dc2d-4148-9c47-acb8e7589c33
3  2020/02/10/[$LATEST]85c744cede7f405997aff8198ce0604e 2020-02-10T13:01:44.718000 REPORT RequestId:
   ↪   6b2b4dc3-dc2d-4148-9c47-acb8e7589c33  Duration: 19.64 mBilled Duration: 100 ms      Memory Size:
   ↪   128 MB Max Memory Used: 46 MB
```

For more information on these and other `sam logs` options, see the SAM Logs Command Reference[1] page.

> ## SAM usually shows only recent logs
>
> Unless you ask for a specific time segment, `sam logs` shows only messages logged in the previous 10 minutes. To show older messages, specify a starting point with -s. You can also restrict the end of the message period with the -e option. Provide a relative value such as '5mins ago' or a specific time in the format 'YYYY-MM-DD HH:MM:SS'.

Searching logs

Remote execution logs, especially for busy services, tend to contain a lot of data. If you are looking for a specific entry, you can save time by telling SAM to automatically search logs and display only messages matching a keyword. To do that, use the --filter option. For example, the following command will show only the log lines containing the word ERROR from the last month:

```
sam logs -n HelloWorldFunction --stack-name sam-test-1 --filter ERROR -s "1 month ago"
```

Search filters do not have to be simple keywords; they can include logical operators and even deep inspection of JSON structures. For more information on the syntax for filters, check out the Filter and Pattern Syntax[2] page in the CloudWatch user guide.

SAM will retrieve messages from all the log streams associated with the specified function and show the stream identifier in the first column of the results (in the previous listing, all the logs are in the same stream: 2020/02/10/[$LATEST]85c744cede7f405997aff8198ce0604e). To look at only a single stream, either filter the messages based on the stream identifier or use the `aws logs` command instead of `sam logs`.

The `aws logs` command does not make any assumptions about working with CloudFormation stacks or functions, but instead lets you access CloudWatch structures directly, so it might be helpful for more complex queries. This command has several tools, including filter-log-events, which retrieves remote logs and allows searching for CloudWatch log events by a full stream name or a prefix. When using `aws logs` instead of `sam logs`, you will need to provide a full log group name instead of just a function name. Lambda creates log groups for functions by adding the /aws/lambda/ prefix to the physical name, so a function called sam-test-1-HelloWorldFunction-1WILG175MZ3XV would log events to the group /aws/lambda/sam-test-1-HelloWorldFunction-1WILG175MZ3XV.

To see all the options, run the following command:

```
aws logs filter-log-events help
```

---

[1]https://docs.aws.amazon.com/serverless-application-model/latest/developerguide/sam-cli-command-reference-sam-logs.html

[2]https://docs.aws.amazon.com/AmazonCloudWatch/latest/logs/FilterAndPatternSyntax.html

Logging incoming events

An amazingly useful option of `sam logs` is `--tail`. It will continuously check for updates and show new log outputs as they appear. Remember that CloudWatch isn't pulling information from a single source, so the tail operation isn't synchronous, but it is generally quick enough for troubleshooting.

Let's try it out. Run the `sam logs` command in tail mode and keep it open. We'll add some more logging to the function so you can see the outputs.

```
sam logs -n HelloWorldFunction --stack-name sam-test-1 --tail
```

Next, open the function source code from `hello-world/app.js` and add a line to log the event details just below the function start (add line 3 from the following listing into your function):

—————————————————————— ch4/hello-world/app.js ——————————————————————

```
1  let response;
2  exports.lambdaHandler = async (event, context) => {
3    console.log(JSON.stringify(event, null, 2));
```

> You'll notice that the header name in the previous listing points to ch4. The tutorial files evolve through chapters in this book, and the final version at the end of each chapter is in a separate directory of the source code package at https://runningserverless.com. If you started from scratch, just ignore the chapter prefix and keep editing the `hello-world/app.js` file. If you want to skip steps from the tutorial, chapter versions make it easy to start from a specific point in the tutorial or inspect solutions.

Build, package and deploy the function again. Check out Chapter 3 if you need a refresher on how to do this. When the deployment completes, reload the web page that triggers the Lambda function (you can find it in your stack outputs). You should see a JSON object for the request appear in the console window where you are tailing the logs.

This is a very useful pattern for inspecting the format of incoming events. Various AWS services all have their own event formats when invoking Lambda functions, and I usually first just log the event to the console to see how to extract important information.

Simulating Lambda locally

Deploying a new version of a Lambda function takes only a minute or two, which is amazing when you consider how many things need to be created in the background, but this is still too slow for a smooth development flow. Together with Docker, SAM can also simulate the Lambda runtime environment locally, so you can experiment and debug code much faster than when deploying to AWS.

Run the following command from your project directory (app), which contains the application template (template.yaml):

```
sam local start-api
```

This should start up a local API Gateway emulation and a local Lambda execution environment, and print out the details:

```
1   $ sam local start-api
2   2020-02-10 15:22:17 Found credentials in shared credentials file: ~/.aws/credentials
3   2020-02-10 15:22:17 Mounting HelloWorldFunction at http://127.0.0.1:3000/hello [GET]
4   2020-02-10 15:22:17 You can now browse to the above endpoints to invoke your functions. You do not
    ↪  need to restart/reload SAM CLI while working on your functions, changes will be reflected
    ↪  instantly/automatically. You only need to restart SAM CLI if you update your AWS SAM template
5   2020-02-10 15:22:17 * Running on http://127.0.0.1:3000/ (Press CTRL+C to quit)
```

If you get an error complaining that Docker is not installed (for example '*Error: Running AWS SAM projects locally requires Docker. Have you got it installed?*'), check if your Docker Desktop software is running. SAM needs Docker to simulate the Lambda environment locally. The error will complain about Docker not being installed even it it is installed but just not running.

Check the URL printed in the console and add hello to it (the sample template maps a Lambda function to the /hello URL). Based on the log (see line 5 in the previous listing), the URL should be http://127.0.0.1:3000/hello. Open the URL in your browser, and you should see the function running.

SAM downloads Docker images

To save disk space, SAM skips downloading the Docker images for simulating Lambda runtimes during initial installation. The first time you try to execute a function in a simulated runtime, it will retrieve the relevant image and store it locally. This means that the initial request might take a while to execute. Subsequent requests will be quick, though.

This simulation will automatically reload the function code if you rebuild the project. For example, open hello-world/app.js and change the message from hello world to something else. Then run sam build in a different command line window (keep the simulated function running), and reload the browser window. You should see the updated message.

You can also use sam local to send events to individual Lambda functions (even for stacks that do not have an API Gateway component). To do that, use invoke followed by the logical name of the function from the stack template. If you do not specify an event from the command line, SAM will wait for the event on the console input. Alternatively, you can pass --event followed by a file name containing the test event.

Now that we're logging incoming events, it's easy to just take sample events from remote CloudWatch logs and replay them locally in a simulated environment for debugging. List the logs, copy an event (look for a JSON structure), and then save it to event.json.

Run the following command from the project directory (app) to send the event to the function running in the simulated Lambda environment:

```
sam local invoke HelloWorldFunction --event event.json
```

Debugging functions

Because Lambda functions run on an auto-scaling architecture, and users don't really control how many instances run at any given time, it's not possible to debug them remotely. However, because of the transient nature of Lambda functions, it's relatively easy to debug functions locally. We can capture remote events, for example from logs, as in the previous section, and replay them in a local environment. SAM command line tools can also generate test events for popular services, so you do not have to capture them from logs. For more information, check out the section *Generating test events* in Chapter 9.

Of course, we could send an event directly to the function handler from an integrated development environment (IDE) or a unit testing tool. That is a great option for quick experiments or even automated regression tests. For more integrated tests, using SAM local invocation becomes incredibly useful. You can pass -d followed by a port number, and SAM will set up a debug session on the specified port; you can then use standard remote debugging tools. At the time when I wrote this, SAM supported debugging JavaScript, Python and GO code. If your functions are for a different runtime, you will still be able to invoke them locally, but may not be able to debug them. For up-to-date information on debugging support, check out the page Step-through Debugging Lambda Functions Locally[3] in the AWS SAM developer guide.

For JavaScript runtimes, SAM sets up the debugging session with the Node.js Inspector protocol. Most IDE tools can connect to that debugging session as well as the Google Chrome DevTools (Figure 4.5). For example, the following command would launch a debugging session on port 8080 and send an event saved in the previous section:

```
sam local invoke HelloWorldFunction --event event.json -d 8080
```

To open a debugging session in Google Chrome development tools, open the special chrome://inspect page in the Chrome browser then add the local machine address and debugging port (the one specified using the -d option when launching sam) in the list of available network targets. Chrome will then provide a link to the active debugging session. For more information on debugging Node.js applications, including how to launch the debugger with other tools, check out the Node.js Inspector documentation[4]. The debug option also works with start-api, but it can only attach a single function to the debugger at a time. You will need to initiate an HTTPS request to an API endpoint connected with a Lambda function before SAM activates a debugging session.

Using sam local and Docker makes the development flow significantly faster than deploying everything to AWS. Note, however, that the emulation is not perfect, so you may run into errors locally related to security roles and access to third party resources for code that works perfectly fine when deployed to Lambda.

---

[3]https://docs.aws.amazon.com/serverless-application-model/latest/developerguide/serverless-sam-cli-using-debugging.html
[4]https://nodejs.org/en/docs/inspector

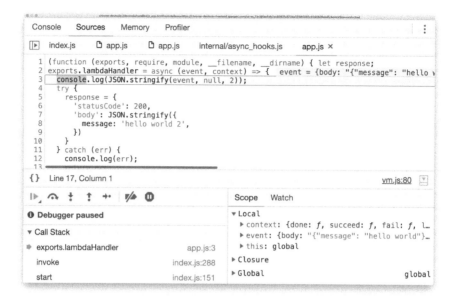

Figure 4.5: *Chrome DevTools can connect to the debugging session set up by SAM.*

Validating templates

YAML makes it easy to read CloudFormation template files, but is very fiddly and error prone. Small spacing issues can cause problems, and that might not be immediately obvious when you read a template. Cloud-Formation will try deploying resources even when the template is not fully valid, and then fail when it starts processing an invalid resource, so feedback on errors might take a long time with complex templates. One of the projects I work on includes custom DNS setup for a content delivery distribution, which takes about 35-40 minutes to fully set up. Messing around with a template where you can only find out if it's correct or not after 40 minutes is a great way to lose a whole day just fixing a tiny issue.

Instead of waiting for CloudFormation to explode on invalid templates, use CFN Lint[5] to perform basic validation locally. CFN Lint understands CloudFormation resources, so is smart enough to catch it when you mistype a property name. Install CFN Lint locally using the following command:

```
pip install cfn-lint
```

You can then check the basic syntax of your templates from the command line easily:

```
$ cfn-lint template.yaml
E0001 Resource with id [HelloWorldFunction] is invalid. property Hanler not defined for resource of
    type AWS::Serverless::Function
code/basic-template/template.yaml:1:1
```

---

[5]https://github.com/awslabs/cfn-python-lint

CFN Lint also integrates nicely into popular code editors, so you can get feedback as you edit the template code (Figure 4.6). It's not perfect, for example it will not catch a misnamed resource, but it will save you a ton of time when experimenting with CloudFormation and SAM.

```
 9  Globals:
10    Function:
11      Timeout: 3
12
13  Resources:
14
15    HelloWorldFunction:
16      Type: AWS::Serverless::Function
17      Properties:
18        CodeUri: hello-world/
19        Hander: app.lambdaHandler
20        Runtime: nodejs8.10
21        Events:
22          HelloWorld:
23            Type: Api
24            Properties:
25              Path: /hello
[1] template.yaml [Syntax: line:1 (1)]                    [cloudformation] utf-8 47% 19:9
 1 Resource with id [HelloWorldFunction] is invalid. property Hander not defined for res

~
~
~
~

[Location List] :SyntasticCheck cfn_lint (cloudformation)              1,1-63          All
-- VISUAL LINE --                                                         1
```

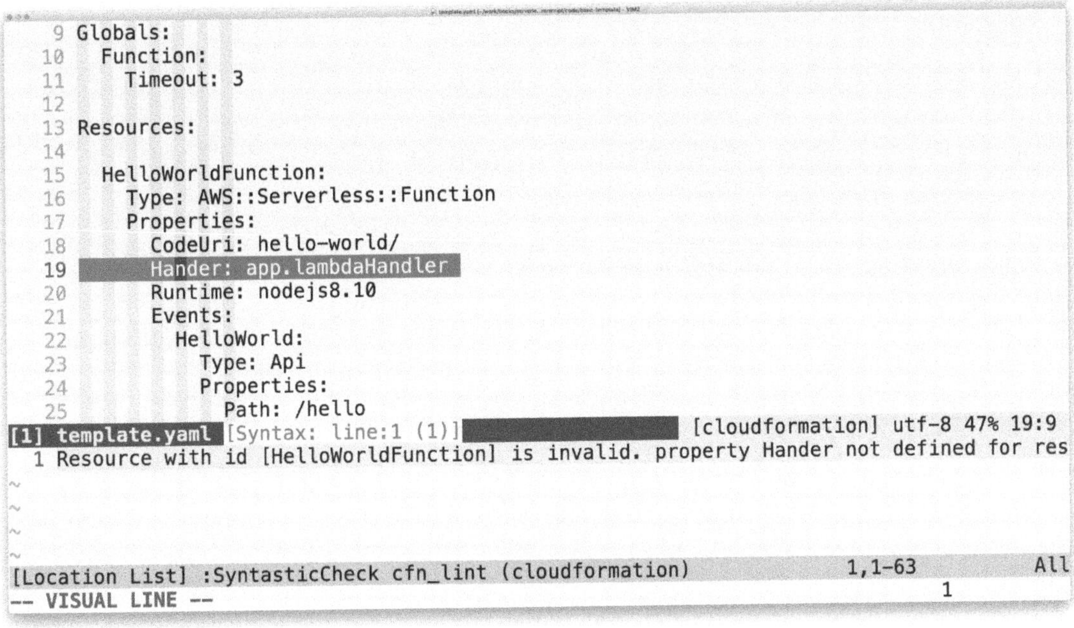

Figure 4.6: *CFN lint saves us from simple typos.*

AWS resources have many optional configuration properties, and CFN Lint won't complain if YAML formatting issues turn an optional parameter into a non-existent value (wrong indentation is a common culprit). To complement CFN Lint, use yamllint[6] for YAML or eslint[7] for JSON to check for such generic formatting mistakes.

SAM validation

The SAM command line tool also has a validation utility, sam validate. CFN Lint executes SAM validation internally, so it checks for both CloudFormation and SAM errors.

---

[6]https://github.com/adrienverge/yamllint
[7]https://eslint.org/

Working in a team

Modern cloud-based applications usually rely on a whole host of platform services, requiring remote resources for reliable integration testing. When a team of developers work on the same application, it's necessary to somehow isolate remote resources, especially for testing purposes, so people can avoid overwriting each other's work.

There are several possible ways of isolating resources with AWS SAM:

- Create multiple stacks in a single account.
- Use different virtual private clouds.
- Use different AWS accounts.

CloudFormation brings up an entire application using a single command, including remote resources and all the required configuration. To create an individual copy of the application, just change the name of the stack in the `sam deploy` command, and SAM will bring up a completely new instance of everything instead of updating an old environment. Using separate stacks for development, testing and production is a very common way to organise resources for a small team. This approach also makes it easy for developers to set up their own copies of the application for testing, in effect creating a CloudFormation stack for each developer.

Small teams usually keep everything under the same AWS account, sometimes even using the same access keys for development and deployment. That is easy and convenient, but doesn't really prevent people from messing up. AWS supports complex authentication and authorisation policies, so larger organisations often want to isolate developer resources directly on AWS. Many organisations want to isolate production environment access, so that developer keys can't be used to arbitrarily poke around the deployed application for end users. The usual reasons for this are data security and auditability. Even if you do not work in a regulated environment requiring strong data protection, it's a good practice to isolate production keys to prevent accidental errors.

For container-based applications, organisations often set up different access keys for each environment or even each developer, and then apply access policies to those keys so people can update only their own resources. This is relatively difficult to do with CloudFormation and SAM. Because CloudFormation generates resource names automatically, it's not easy to set up name-based access policies for resources. Using SAM will ensure that each stack you deploy is completely isolated, but it will not prevent someone unintentionally deleting the wrong stack.

A much more convenient solution for isolation with CloudFormation and SAM is to set up separate AWS account deployments. Each AWS account has completely separate resources, without even the need to apply different IAM policies. Until relatively recently it was difficult to manage multiple accounts, but you can now easily create sub-accounts from the AWS Organisations Console[8]. To deploy a stack using a specific account, create a profile using `aws configure` then just add the profile name after `--profile` to `sam package` and `sam deploy`. The `sam build` works locally, so you do not have to run it separately for different profiles.

---

[8]https://console.aws.amazon.com/organizations/home

Setting up a deployment pipeline

So far, we've always executed the build and deploy commands from a single computer, with the same AWS account used for development. If you work alone or in a very small team, that deployment flow is probably good enough. For an even slightly larger group, you'll probably want to set up a deployment pipeline.

The purpose of a pipeline is to reduce errors by making software releases reproducible and reliable. A deployment pipeline does that by orchestrating the work required to convert source code into a fully deployed application, automating repetitive and error prone tasks. The deployment tasks usually involve downloading a clean version of the source code, running automated tests, producing application binaries or package artefacts, and installing the application in approval or release environments (Figure 4.7). Some of those steps might also involve manual approval, requiring humans to verify release candidates or perform additional manual tests.

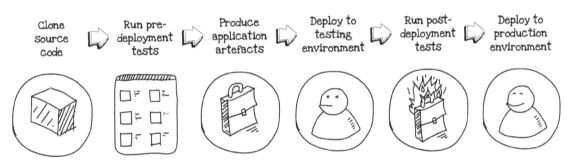

Figure 4.7: *Delivery pipelines orchestrate tasks to convert source code into a fully deployed application.*

A delivery pipeline is closely tied to the workflow of a particular team. It depends on a mix of technology choices including source code repositories and programming language specific build systems, but also on company or team policies for source code branching, testing procedures and deployment authorisations. Fully covering all important options for deployment pipelines is outside the scope of this section, as that topic itself would likely require longer than this whole book. In this section we'll focus on what's important for pipelines using AWS SAM.

SAM provides convenient tools for development and deployment tasks (Figure 3.2), explained in Chapter 3. In the context of most deployment pipelines, running sam build and sam package steps is sufficient to create deployment artefacts (Figure 4.8). Unlike typical deployment pipelines where compiled code packages pass between steps, sam package already uploads deployable Lambda function archives to an S3 bucket, so you don't have to worry about storing those. During the packaging step, SAM will replace local paths from the input template with uploaded package URLs and store the results in an output template (in the previous chapter we used output.yaml). Your pipeline needs to keep the output file produced by the packaging step and make it available to CloudFormation during deployment steps.

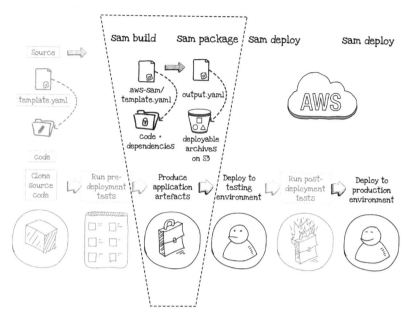

Figure 4.8: *SAM tools for building and packaging can be used to create application artefacts in a delivery pipeline. The SAM deployment tool can be used to create testing and production environments.*

If you're starting from scratch and you don't mind hosting everything inside AWS, check out AWS CodeStar[9]. CodeStar is a visual interface for setting up a full project development environment in AWS, including source code hosting, build systems and deployment pipelines. It integrates nicely with Cloud-Formation and AWS SAM, and will allow you to set up a relatively standard delivery pipeline in just a few clicks.

If you want to host code somewhere outside AWS, but want to run the deployment pipeline inside AWS, consider using AWS CodePipeline[10]. It's a continuous delivery pipeline management system with a convenient wizard setup process, allowing you to define packaging and build steps in a few clicks. The benefit of using CodePipeline is that authentication to access other AWS resources is trivial to set up, since it's all controlled by IAM. (CodeStar will actually set up a CodePipeline instance for you.) When using CodePipeline, instead of sam deploy, use the built-in AWS CloudFormation deployment provider for CodePipeline and point it to the output template generated by sam package.

If you're using a different pipeline product, be sure to upload the output template to S3 after the packaging step. CloudFormation can directly deploy from templates on S3, so just upload the template to the same bucket where sam package is sending function code packages. Instead of sam deploy, use aws cloudformation update-stack and point it to the URL of your output template using --template-url.

Regardless of the delivery pipeline product you use, creating a separate account for the pipeline is the easiest way to nicely isolate environments. With CodePipeline you don't even have to generate API access keys, as it will manage everything through IAM policies assigned to the sub-account.

---

[9]https://aws.amazon.com/codestar/
[10]https://aws.amazon.com/codepipeline/

Using a single pipeline account would isolate development and deployment access keys, preventing developers from accidentaly touching production resources. However, the same pipeline AWS account would own the testing and production environments. This is usually fine for small and medium-size organisations. Large corporations often want to isolate production environments from any testing resources, for security reasons and to catch cross-account isolation problems during testing.

To fully isolate application resources, it's best to create a separate AWS account for each environment. Multi-account pipelines are, by design, much more complex than single-account pipelines. Different resources belong to different accounts, so tasks can't just reuse outputs of other tasks. To avoid rebuilding everything from scratch at every step of your pipeline, consider creating a common S3 bucket for the artefact repository and allowing all the sub-accounts read-only access to that bucket. Check out the page How can I provide cross-account access to objects that are in Amazon S3 buckets?[11] from AWS support for more information on the required IAM policies for this kind of setup. The start of the pipeline can produce application artefacts by running sam package and uploading the executable Lambda packages to the common S3 bucket, and all the other sub-accounts can use sam deploy to create their own resources. Be sure to also upload the resulting CloudFormation template (output.yaml in the previous examples) to the artefact repository.

SAM can also help with deployments by automatically configuring AWS resources for gradual roll-outs. This makes it easy to run multiple versions of an application at the same time and direct traffic from the old version to the new one gradually. We'll look into that in the next chapter.

Interesting experiments

- Modify your Lambda function to throw an error, and then deploy and invoke it. Check the Lambda monitoring web console and CloudWatch logs to see how they captured the error information.
- Start tailing the remote logs then fix and deploy the function again. Reload the API web page to invoke the function again and confirm that the fix works in the logs.
- Set up CFN Lint for your favourite code editor then break the template and see how the error gets highlighted.

---

[11]https://aws.amazon.com/premiumsupport/knowledge-center/cross-account-access-s3/

5. Safe deployments

This chapter explains two core features of AWS Lambda, versions and aliases. You will also learn how to use aliases to protect against unexpected deployment problems.

Although AWS Lambda technically works like a virtualised container management system, the life-cycle for Lambda functions is quite different from that of the usual container-based applications. This might be counter-intuitive to people who used managed container services. Luckily, AWS SAM hides most of the underlying complexity from developers. In this chapter, we peek under the hood just enough so you can avoid subtle mistakes. Knowing how Lambda routes requests and provisions runtime environments is also critical for getting the most out of cloud functions.

In the previous chapter, we deployed a new version of the example stack to add logging. New code was available and responding to user requests almost immediately after the deployment. This can give the wrong impression that Lambda works similarly to application hosting services such as App Engine or Heroku. With application hosts, a new deployment typically uploads code to running containers or sets up new instances with the updated code and then destroys the old containers. However, a Lambda deployment does not create or destroy any containers. It only creates a new *function configuration*.

Function configurations

The core principle of serverless work is that the platform is responsible for receiving events from clients, not your code. The network socket (*server*) belongs to the hosting provider, not to your function. This allows the platform to decide how many instances to run and when. Lambda will not start any containers for your function until it receives events for it (unless you explicitly provisioned concurrency). Once related events arrive, the platform will start and maintain enough instances to handle the workload. After a period of inactivity, if no events ask for a particular function, Lambda will remove inactive containers. Although as a user you do not have any control over this process, it's relatively easy to prove it: just measure request latency to spot cold starts.

That process is common for all serverless platform providers. With AWS Lambda in particular, events do not target a particular function. They target a particular version of a function, or, more precisely, events are connected to a version of the function configuration. In the Lambda terminology, the *function configuration* describes all the properties of a runtime environment necessary to spin up a new container. That includes the following:

- The runtime type and version (so far we have used Node 12, but this could be a version of Python, Java, Ruby and so on)
- How much memory and time the function can use
- The URL of the function code package (SAM will set this up on S3 for you during deployment)
- The IAM role specifying what this function can access in AWS and who can call this function
- Error recovery, logging and environment parameters of the function

You can see the configuration for any Lambda function by using the AWS CLI tools. First, find the actual name of the function by listing the stack resources (replace <STACK_NAME> with your stack name):

```
aws cloudformation list-stack-resources --stack-name <STACK_NAME>
```

In the results, find the physical ID associated with a resource of type AWS::Lambda::Function. For example, in the following output listing, the name of the function is on line 6:

```
$ aws cloudformation list-stack-resources --stack-name sam-test-1
{
  "StackResourceSummaries": [
    {
      "LogicalResourceId": "HelloWorldFunction",
      "PhysicalResourceId": "sam-test-1-HelloWorldFunction-QL5VEY42DZ2C",
      "ResourceType": "AWS::Lambda::Function",
      "LastUpdatedTimestamp": "2020-01-16T08:58:53.841Z",
      "ResourceStatus": "UPDATE_COMPLETE"
    },
```

Now that we know the function name, it's easy to look up the details of the configuration. Use the following command line, and replace the placeholder <NAME> with the physical resource ID from the previous listing:

```
aws lambda get-function-configuration --function-name <NAME>
```

Here's an example of the output for my stack:

```
$ aws lambda get-function-configuration --function-name sam-test-1-HelloWorldFunction-QL5VEY42DZ2C
{
  "FunctionName": "sam-test-1-HelloWorldFunction-QL5VEY42DZ2C",
  "FunctionArn": "arn:aws:lambda:us-east-1::function:sam-test-1-HelloWorldFunction-QL5VEY42DZ2C",
  "Runtime": "nodejs12.x",
  "Role": "arn:aws:iam::818931230230:role/sam-test-1-HelloWorldFunctionRole-EGC56VNRV60R",
  "Handler": "app.lambdaHandler",
  "CodeSize": 139311,
  "Description": "",
  "Timeout": 3,
  "MemorySize": 128,
  "LastModified": "2020-01-16T08:58:59.445+0000",
  "CodeSha256": "Do1A72psYkZwFIYHHVkl60Vxst2Z70aqWTjlB+GMVN8=",
  "Version": "$LATEST",
  "TracingConfig": {
      "Mode": "PassThrough"
  },
  "RevisionId": "a9b28347-35b7-41b7-a7cf-2408173d6f49"
}
```

Notice the Version property on line 14. The value $LATEST is a special key, assigned by Lambda to the default configuration version. When we run sam deploy, Lambda only needs to update this configuration; it does not really need to start up or stop any containers.

As an experiment, try extracting the version automatically using the --query and --output parameters as explained in the section *Inspecting a stack from the command line* in Chapter 3. For extra points, try combining all the commands into a single line that only requires the stack name argument.

Versions and aliases

When we deployed the example stack, SAM wired the API gateway to use the $LATEST version of our Lambda function. That's OK for a simple case, but it might be problematic for backwards incompatible deployments in the future. Updating a distributed architecture is not instantaneous. We don't want the API somehow to get updated first then send a new version of an event to an older version of the function Lambda and API Gateway charge for requests, not for the number of environments, so there is no special cost for keeping an old copy around while the new one is being created. With container-based application hosts, the only solution to this problem would be to create a completely different stack and then switch request routing on the load balancer to the new environment at the end of deployment. With Lambda, it's easy to do that even with a single stack.

You can tell Lambda to keep a configuration version by publishing it. *Published versions* are read-only copies of function configurations, and they are not wiped out after a subsequent update. An event source can request that a particular published function version handles its events. That way, old deployments of the API Gateway can ask for the old Lambda code, and new deployments can ask for the new Lambda function. During an update, any events aimed at the previous version will just keep running on old containers. Once no events have requested an old version for a while, Lambda will remove those instances. When an event comes targeting the new version, Lambda will create a new container using the newly published configuration.

To make deployments safe, we need to make sure that events target a particular version, not $LATEST. Each published configuration version has a unique numerical ID, assigned by Lambda incrementally with each deployment. In theory, we could manually keep track of these, ensure that event sources request a particular numerical version, and update the template before each deployment to rewire event sources, but this would be error prone and laborious. Lambda allows us to declare configuration *aliases*, meaningful names pointing to a numerical version. For example, we can create an alias called live to represent a published configuration version, and set up all event sources to request that alias. After an application update, we do not need to rewire event sources. We just need to point the alias to the new numerical version (Figure 5.1).

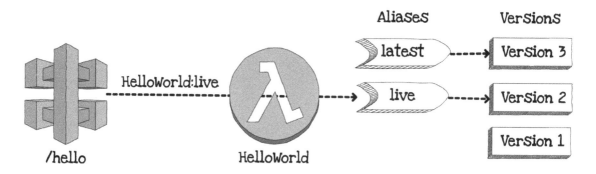

Figure 5.1: *An event source can ask for a specific alias, which points to a numerical version of a function.*

SAM automates the whole process of publishing numerical versions, assigning aliases, and wiring event sources to aliases. All you need to do is add the AutoPublishAlias property to the function properties, followed by the alias. An alias can be any Latin alphanumeric text between 1 and 128 characters.

Let's make deployments safer by using an alias for our HelloWorldFunction. Change template.yaml and add AutoPublishAlias to the function properties, at the same indentation level as Runtime. Give the alias a meaningful name. For example, in the listing below, the alias will be live (see line 17).

—————————————————— ch5/template.yaml ——————————————————

```
HelloWorldFunction:
  Type: AWS::Serverless::Function
  Properties:
    CodeUri: hello-world/
    Handler: app.lambdaHandler
    Runtime: nodejs12.x
    AutoPublishAlias: live
```

Note that you do not need to change the alias name for each deployment. SAM will automatically publish a new numerical version and then reassign the existing alias to it.

SAM versions or CloudFormation versions?

CloudFormation has a low-level resource for Lambda versions (AWS::Lambda::Version), but at the time when I wrote this, it was almost useless. In order to create it, you'd need to specify the SHA256 hash of the latest deployed version, which you generally won't know before deployment. You also can't get it during deployment of a Lambda function, because the CloudFormation Lambda resource does not expose it in any way. The SAM resource using AutoPublishAlias is much simpler and more useful.

Let's create two published versions. Run sam build, sam package and sam deploy with the usual parameters, to create the first published version of the function configuration. Then, so you can see the difference easily, open hello-world/app.js and change the response message (for example, change it to hello world 2). After that build, package and deploy the function again.

You can see the versions and aliases in the AWS Web Console for your Lambda function:

1. Open the AWS Web Console at https://aws.amazon.com and sign in if necessary.
2. Navigate to the Lambda service.
3. Find the HelloWorld function and open the function configuration page.
4. Click on the *Qualifiers* drop down and switch to the *Versions* tab within the drop-down list.

We deployed the stack twice, which created two versions, so you should see two published versions of your function in the *Versions* tab, and the alias live assigned to the second version (Figure 5.2).

You can also get a list of configuration versions from the command line using the following command:

```
aws lambda list-versions-by-function --function-name <NAME>
```

When an event source wants to invoke a function, it can specify a particular version of the configuration it needs, either by providing the configuration number or by specifying an alias.

Figure 5.2: *See the versions and aliases of your Lambda function in the* Qualifiers *drop-down of the Lambda Web Console.*

When an `AWS::Serverless::Function` template includes the `AutoPublishAlias` property, SAM will automatically configure all event sources specified inside the resource to request that particular alias. For event sources specified outside the function resource, you can invoke an alias or a specific version by adding a colon and qualifier after the function name. For example, instead of directly targeting `sam-test-1-HelloWorldFunction-QL5VEY42DZ2C`, configure the event source to connect to version 1 by using the target `sam-test-1-HelloWorldFunction-QL5VEY42DZ2C:1`.

By default, an AWS account has 75 GB available for storing Lambda functions, including the code for all published versions. SAM will not automatically clean up old versions for you, so you may need to periodically do some housekeeping if you deploy large packages frequently. On the other hand, any versions that you do not explicitly delete will be instantly available in the future. Unlike application hosts where rolling back to a previous version requires another deployment, switching back and forth between versions with Lambda can be almost instant. You can also use old published versions for as long as you want.

For example, you can invoke the function directly using the following command:

```
aws lambda invoke --function-name <NAME> <OUTPUT FILE NAME>
```

Note that, unlike the `sam local invoke` command used in the previous chapter, `aws lambda invoke` sends an event to the function deployed to AWS. This will execute the Lambda function, print out the execution status, and save the function output in the specified output file. Print out the file contents to see the actual response:

```
1  $ aws lambda invoke --function-name sam-test-1-HelloWorldFunction-QL5VEY42DZ2C result.txt
2  {
3    "StatusCode": 200,
4    "ExecutedVersion": "$LATEST"
5  }
6
7  $ cat result.txt
8  {"statusCode":200,"body":"{\"message\":\"hello world 2\"}"}
```

Because we did not provide a specific version, the ExecutedVersion (on line 4 of the previous listing) shows
$LATEST. Now specify the previous version using --qualifier:

```
1  $ aws lambda invoke --function-name sam-test-1-HelloWorldFunction-QL5VEY42DZ2C --qualifier 1
↳    result.txt
2  {
3      "StatusCode": 200,
4      "ExecutedVersion": "1"
5  }
6
7  $ cat result.txt
8  {"statusCode":200,"body":"{\"message\":\"hello world\"}"}
```

You can now see that the executed version was 1 (line 4), and that the function response contained the old
message.

In the CloudWatch logs, you can see which version was invoked at the start of each request execution (the
entry will contain the word START). Log streams will also contain the version in square brackets, so you can
easily filter all logs for a particular version.

```
1  $ sam logs -n HelloWorldFunction --stack-name sam-test-1 --filter START
2  2020-02-16 15:03:02 Found credentials in shared credentials file: ~/.aws/credentials
3  2020/02/16/[$LATEST]b151f67 2020-02-16T14:00:34.908000 START RequestId:
↳    0a892e26-3e07-4b33-8a64-1ec71bc031a8 Version: $LATEST
4  2020/02/16/[1]d261bd3a02304 2020-02-16T14:00:50.080000 START RequestId:
↳    32982750-6d6e-4fc9-a6e0-f00858099291 Version: 1
```

Aliases and deployment pipelines

Although in theory you can set up different aliases for development, testing and production, this is
not easy with CloudFormation and SAM. The more usual pattern is to just set up different stacks.
That way each stack has completely separate functions, and those functions each have their own
versions aliases.

The SAM AutoPublishAlias shortcut is helpful to always reassign the same alias, but does not help
much with managing multiple versions in the same stack. Aliases with SAM are mostly useful to
make deployments safer.

Gradual deployments

An alias always points to some numerical version, but it can point to more than one version at the same time. This becomes incredibly useful for safe deployments. Lambda supports automatic load balancing between versions assigned to the same alias, using a feature called *routing configuration*. Another AWS deployment product, called AWS CodeDeploy, can modify the routing configuration over time to gradually switch aliases between several versions of code and infrastructure. CodeDeploy can, for example, use the new version of an application only for 10% of the traffic and wait for a short period while monitoring for unexpected problems. If everything looks OK, CodeDeploy can expose the new version to everyone and shut down the old version. On the other hand, if the new version seems to be problematic, CodeDeploy will move all the users back to the old infrastructure and destroy the experimental version. Reassigning aliases to published configuration versions is very quick, much faster than a redeployment, making it easy and quick to recover from deployment errors.

SAM automates most of the heavy lifting when setting up gradual deployments. It will automatically create CodeDeploy resources for Lambda functions, set up security permissions, and configure aliases and routing configurations. CloudFormation manages all resources in a template as a group, so if a single function causes gradual deployment to roll back, all the other resources will be automatically restored to the previous compatible state. Because Lambda pricing is based on actual utilisation, not reserved capacity, having a gradual deployment does not cost more than just using a single version. The experimental infrastructure and the old one will split the requests, so the combined utilisation is the same. The only downside to adding gradual deployments is that an application update takes longer, in order to run the experiment and decide whether the new version is good enough to keep.

Application developers just need to define what exactly it means for a deployment to be problematic. For example, we could run an experimental version for a few minutes and check for Lambda errors or time-outs. This is an easy way to prevent integration problems that were not detected during testing. Alternatively, we could run the experiment over a longer period of time and measure user behaviour, such as funnel conversion or purchases. For example, if the unit and integration tests were passed, but something unexpected is causing users to buy less with the new version, would it not be smart to automatically roll back and protect revenue, and alert someone to investigate it? You can set up those kinds of checks with CodeDeploy.

Modifying routing configuration manually

SAM only manages routing configuration for deployments. If you want to play with this feature outside deployments, for example to run A/B tests in production, configure the alias routing configuration using the AWS command line tools. Use the `aws lambda update-alias` command. You can do this even for functions created using SAM.

To set up gradual deployment, add the `DeploymentPreference` section to the function properties. This should be on the same indentation level as the other function properties. To avoid formatting issues, add the section immediately below the `AutoPublishAlias`. (Routing configurations only work with aliases, not numerical versions, so the alias configuration needs to stay in the template.)

——————————————— ch5/template.yaml ———————————————

```
DeploymentPreference:
  Type: Linear10PercentEvery1Minute
```

Change the welcome message in hello-world/app.js so you can see the difference between versions (for example, make it hello world 3). Then build, package and deploy the stack again. Note that this deployment will take significantly longer than usual (about 10 minutes), because of the gradual traffic shifting. During deployment, try accessing the web page of your application. You should see the old message nine out of 10 times, but the new message should also show occasionally. The deployment should last roughly 10 minutes. As the traffic shifts, the new message should show up more frequently.

SAM command line tools do not provide any indication about gradual deployment progress, but you can see traffic shifting in action in the AWS Web Console. Find the application stack in the AWS CloudFormation Web Console during deployment, and open the *Events* tab. Within the messages, you'll see that SAM created a CodeDeploy application, a CodeDeploy resource group and a service role for deployment (Figure 5.3).

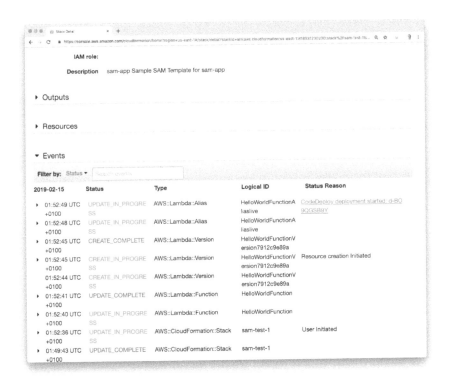

Figure 5.3: *CloudFormation console shows a link to a CodeDeploy task in progress.*

Look for an UPDATE_IN_PROGRESS message for AWS::Lambda::Alias in the list of events. There should be a hyperlink in the same row as that message, with the text starting with CodeDeploy deployment started. Click the link and you'll see the status of your gradual deployment (Figure 5.4).

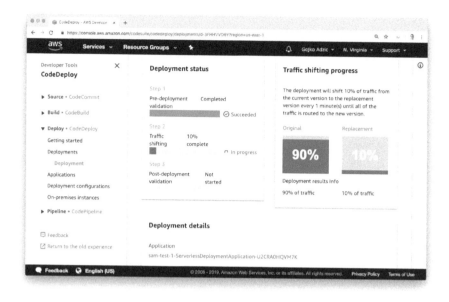

Figure 5.4: *CodeDeploy has started sending a small percentage of requests to the new version.*

CodeDeploy only works with existing aliases

If you set up aliases and CodeDeploy during the same deployment, CodeDeploy won't do much initially, because it relies on updating an existing alias and shifting traffic from the old version associated with it. This is why we first created an alias and then added a deployment preference in this chapter.

The Type property inside DeploymentPreference controls how the traffic moves from the old to the new version. SAM can automate two types of deployment preference: linear and canary.

Linear deployments work by incrementally moving traffic during a period of time. In this example, we set it to Linear10PercentEvery1Minute. This, unsurprisingly, turns on the tap slightly more every minute, so that the new version starts with only 10% of the requests and each minute gets 10% more. That is why the new message will show up more frequently as the deployment progresses.

Canary deployments work in two steps. At the start of the deployment, CodeDeploy sets up routing so that the new version gets a specific percentage of requests. If there are no problems until the end of the deployment, the alias is completely assigned to the new version. For example, Canary10Percent15Minutes would send 10% of the traffic to the new version at the start, wait 15 minutes, and then move the remaining 90% to the new version. See the AWS Documentation page on Gradual Code Deployments[1] for an up-to-date list of all the deployment preference types.

---

[1]https://docs.aws.amazon.com/serverless-application-model/latest/developerguide/automating-updates-to-serverless-apps.html

Adding deployment alerts

So far, we're not really testing anything to compare the old and the new version. We could manually try things out during the deployment and then roll back in case of problems from the CodeDeploy Web Console, but that's not really efficient or sustainable. It would be better if CodeDeploy did this automatically.

Luckily, CloudWatch can look out for errors automatically. We used CloudWatch to access logs in the previous chapter, but we can also use it to inspect and monitor operational statistics about our application. CloudWatch automatically tracks lots of interesting information about AWS Lambda and API Gateway, such as latency, number of invocations and number of errors (Figure 5.5). Here is how you can see this information:

1. Go to the AWS Web Console, https://aws.amazon.com, and sign in if necessary.
2. Select *CloudWatch* in the list of services.
3. Select *Metrics* in the left-hand menu.
4. In the list of metric namespaces, select *Lambda* then *By Function name*, and select check boxes next to errors and invocations for your function.

Figure 5.5: *CloudWatch automatically tracks useful operational metrics for Lambda functions and API Gateway resources.*

Monitoring changes over time might be interesting and even amusing, but we should not rely on human interaction to spot errors. CloudWatch can automatically send notifications if metrics exceed some thresholds, using a feature called *alarms*. We could set up an alarm to send someone an email in case user requests start taking too long to execute, or even invoke a Lambda function when something bad happens.

To create an alarm manually, switch to the *Graphed metrics* tab, then click the bell icon in the *Actions* column next to a metric row in the bottom table on the page. You can, for example, use that to send yourself an email if a Lambda function starts throwing errors.

Of course, we can also set up alarms directly in a CloudFormation template. SAM does not have any specific shortcuts for that, so we'll just use the standard AWS::CloudWatch::Alarm[2] resource. Add the block from the following listing to your application template, in the Resources section (it should be at the same indentation level as HelloWorldFunction).

──────────────────── ch5/template.yaml ────────────────────

```
29  HelloWorldErrors:
30    Type: AWS::CloudWatch::Alarm
31    Properties:
32      MetricName: Errors
33      Statistic: Sum
34      ComparisonOperator: GreaterThanThreshold
35      Threshold: 5
36      Period: 60
37      EvaluationPeriods: 1
38      TreatMissingData: notBreaching
39      Namespace: "AWS/Lambda"
40      Dimensions:
41        - Name: FunctionName
42          Value: !Ref HelloWorldFunction
```

The previous resource block will configure an automatic alarm if HelloWorldFunction (lines 39-42) reports more than five errors (lines 32-35) over 60 seconds (line 36). Note how the alarm refers to another resource in the same template, in line 42. The exclamation mark (!) signals a function call in CloudFormation, and Ref is a function that turns a logical resource ID into its actual physical name. CloudFormation will replace !Ref HelloWorldFunction with the actual function name when it creates the resource.

To tell CodeDeploy to roll back the update in case of problems, we need to add a reference to this alarm in the Alarms list of the function DeploymentPreference. YAML uses dashes (-) to prefix list elements, so we need to add a dash before the reference. We can use !Ref again to convert a logical identifier into an actual resource name.

──────────────────── ch5/template.yaml ────────────────────

```
18  DeploymentPreference:
19    Type: Linear10PercentEvery1Minute
20    Alarms:
21      - !Ref HelloWorldErrors
```

With that change, the deployment configuration will automatically test for Lambda errors and prevent a bad release if early users start getting unexpected integration problems. The nice aspect of the current configuration is that it is completely generic, so you can apply it to all your Lambda functions. The downside is that it just checks for technical errors, not for business problems.

The Alarms property is a list, so we can set up more than one alarm to monitor your deployments. For example, we can add a custom metric to CloudWatch to record sales, then check for unexpected changes in sales

───────────────────────

[2]https://docs.aws.amazon.com/AWSCloudFormation/latest/UserGuide/aws-properties-cw-alarm.html

patterns. CloudWatch alarms can perform some basic statistics on custom metrics to spot trend changes (see the Create a CloudWatch Alarm based on a Metric Math Expression[3] page in the CloudWatch documentation for more information). You can, of course, execute more complex calculations using Lambda functions. For example, instead of sending individual order information to CloudWatch, a Lambda function could add up all sales in one-hour intervals and just submit the difference from the previous period as a CloudWatch metric.

CodeDeploy can also run custom code before or after the deployment, to set up or clean up after tests. Unsurprisingly, this kind of custom integration uses Lambda functions. Use the Hooks property to define a PreTraffic function which will be executed before a gradual deployment, and a PostTraffic function that will be executed after the deployment completes.

Here is an example of a full setup for a DeploymentPreference:

```
DeploymentPreference:
  Type: Canary10Percent10Minutes
  Alarms:
    - !Ref CheckForLambdaErrors
    - !Ref CheckForDropInSales
    - !Ref CheckForDropInConversion
  Hooks:
    PreTraffic: !Ref ClearStatisticsLambda
    PostTraffic: !Ref NotifyAdminsLambda
```

This example is illustrative (the code is not in the source code package for the book), but shows how you could set up the alarms and related Lambda functions to manipulate custom data. I will leave this to you for homework.

Interesting experiments

- In the CloudWatch metrics page, add some interesting metrics for API Gateway and Lambda properties, and inspect what other metrics you can chart for the example application.
- Open the CodeDeploy Web Console during a gradual deployment, and force a deployment roll-back from the user interface. Check the CloudFormation Console to see how the entire stack rolls back.
- Add a second function to the SAM template and set it up with a gradual deployment. Try rolling back just one function, and see how the other behaves.
- Intentionally cause a bug in one of the functions, then deploy again and invoke the broken function enough times to trigger the deployment alarm. Observe how CloudFormation handles that issue.

---

[3]https://docs.aws.amazon.com/AmazonCloudWatch/latest/monitoring/Create-alarm-on-metric-math-expression.html

Part II

Working with AWS services

6. Handling HTTP requests

This chapter explains how to create HTTP APIs and dynamic web pages using Lambda. You'll also learn about customising API Gateway resources and how to pass parameters to CloudFormation templates.

So far, we've mostly looked into managing Lambda functions, but the sample project we deployed in Chapter 3 configured one more resource, the API Gateway. API Gateway is a service for publishing and managing REST and Websocket APIs.

We're currently using it to just pass through requests from client browsers to a Lambda function, but it can do much more. API Gateway can throttle requests to prevent clients from overloading a back-end service, authenticate and authorise requests, enforce usage plans, and even transform or enrich incoming and outgoing payloads. API Gateway does not necessarily have to forward requests to a Lambda function; it could potentially send them to some other web API you host, or to a different AWS service. In the scope of this book, though, we'll always use the Lambda back end.

API Gateway events

If a Lambda function has any Api events associated with it, SAM will create an API Gateway and wire it up to the function. The Events section of the sample template has one such event:

—————————————————————————— template.yaml ——————————————————————————

```
17  Events:
18    HelloWorld:
19      Type: Api
20      Properties:
21        Path: /hello
22        Method: get
```

You can easily find the API Gateway resource that SAM configured for us in the AWS Web Console:

1. Open https://aws.amazon.com and sign in if necessary.
2. Select the CloudFormation service and find the deployed stack (sam-test-1).
3. In the *Resources* tab, look for an item of type AWS::ApiGateway::RestApi and click the hyperlink in that row.

Alternatively, select the *API Gateway* service in the AWS Web Console and find the API with the same name as your stack (if you followed the steps in Chapter 3, this will be sam-test-1).

Swagger API definitions

API Gateway can also support rich API model definitions through Swagger, a popular API configuration framework. This might be useful if you are deploying a service API for strongly typed languages or mobile clients, because you can even generate the client SDK code based on a Swagger template. In this book, though, we'll always use the Proxy integration. JavaScript has no types anyway.

The API Gateway Web Console shows several sections under the API name, such as *Resources*, *Stages* and *Dashboard*. The Dashboard screen (Figure 6.1) shows a quick summary of recent requests, along with basic latency metrics. It might be interesting to see basic operational statistics during troubleshooting.

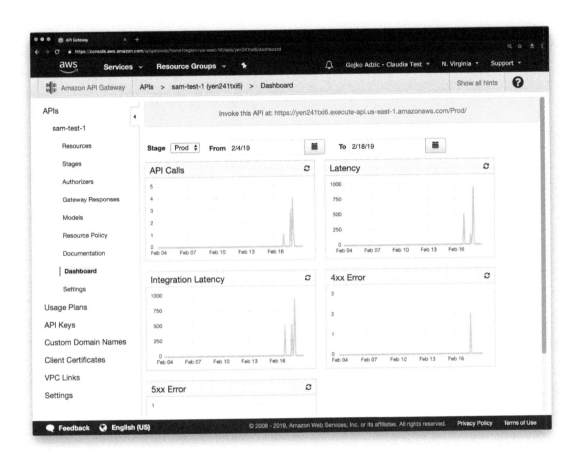

Figure 6.1: *API Gateway Web Console dashboard shows basic operational statistics.*

In the API Gateway terminology, a *resource* is an endpoint configured to handle an HTTP request on a specific path, and with a specific HTTP method. SAM automatically added a single resource based on the Events property of the Lambda function, configured to handle GET requests to the /hello path. Select the *Resources* section in the left menu under your API to see that resource (Figure 6.2).

To keep things simple, SAM did not set up any authentication and did not configure any conversions or transformation for the responses. It just set up API Gateway to pass all the data to Lambda and return back whatever Lambda sends it. This type of integration is called *Lambda Proxy*, which you will be able to see in the *Integration Request* box on the screen of your Web Console (top-right box in Figure 6.2). Note that Lambda proxy responses do not just contain the raw HTML, but also a JSON object with HTTP response information, explained more in the next section.

Figure 6.2: *API Gateway Web Console shows the details of a resource, including the authentication setup and the back end it talks to. It also enables us to send test requests easily.*

Customising responses

API Gateway expects responses in a specific format from Lambda Proxy integrations. The response needs to be a JSON object containing these fields:

- statusCode should be a number, containing the numeric HTTP response code. The number 200 means OK.
- body should be a string, representing the response contents.
- headers is an optional argument, and can contain a map of HTTP response headers.

SAM assumes that we'll use API Gateway to create JSON APIs, so unless the response provides a content type, it assumes that we'll be sending back a serialised JSON object. That's why the sample function formats the response object using JSON.stringify:

―――――――――――――――――― hello-world/app.js ――――――――――――――――――

```
response = {
  'statusCode': 200,
  'body': JSON.stringify({
    message: 'hello world',
  })
}
```

To show you how to customise responses, we'll make API Gateway send back a web page instead of a JSON object. For example, let's create a web form where users will be able to enter their name.

First of all, let's create a utility function that packages up a response containing some text with the correct headers. In this case, we just need to set the Content-Type header to text/html.

―――――――――――――――――― ch6/hello-world/html-response.js ――――――――――――――――――

```
module.exports = function htmlResponse(body) {
  return {
    statusCode: 200,
    body: body,
    headers: {
      'Content-Type': 'text/html'
    }
  };
};
```

We can now change the main Lambda function file (app.js) to return an HTML form easily:

Serving static HTML from Lambda functions is a bad idea

To keep things simple for now, we'll use Lambda functions to send HTML back to web browsers. This is perfectly fine for quick experiments and tutorials, but is far from optimal in a more general case. It's much cheaper and faster to host static files in S3 and combine that with Lambda functions for dynamic responses. We'll use this combination in Chapter 11.

––––––––––––––––––––––––––––––––– ch6/hello-world/app.js –––––––––––––––––––––––––

```js
const htmlResponse = require('./html-response');
const formHtml = `
  <html>
  <head>
    <meta charset="utf-8"/>
  </head>
  <body>
    <form method="POST">
      Please enter your name:
      <input type="text" name="name"/>
      <br/>
      <input type="submit" />
    </form>
  </body>
  </html>
`;
exports.lambdaHandler = async (event, context) => {
  console.log(JSON.stringify(event, null, 2));
  return htmlResponse(formHtml);
};
```

Speed up deployments

We added a deployment preference to the SAM template in the section *Gradual deployments* in Chapter 5. This is great for production-worthy applications, but slows down experimentation unnecessarily for the examples in this chapter. Remove the gradual deployment preference and the associated CloudWatch alert from the template before deploying, so you can test things faster.

Build, package and deploy the stack. Open the API URL again in your browser (you can find it in the Stack outputs), and it should now show a web form, nicely rendered (Figure 6.3).

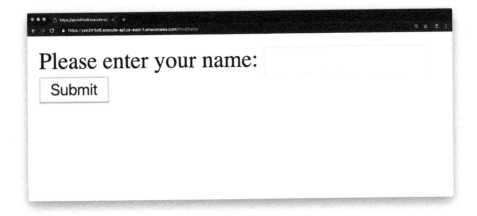

Figure 6.3: *Adding the Content-Type header makes it easy to send back HTML pages from Lambda.*

Try submitting the form and you'll get a 403 Not Authorized response complaining about a missing authentication token. That's because there's no resource in the API Gateway to handle the form submission yet.

Troubleshooting Gateway integrations

API Gateway masks unhandled errors, such as a missing resource, with a 403 Not Authorized response. If anything goes wrong talking to the back-end service, you'll only see that error instead of useful troubleshooting information. This is great from the security perspective, because it prevents sensitive data leaks, but it's a major pain for troubleshooting problems. Here are just some of the cases when you'll see this generic error:

- If the request does not even reach the Lambda function, for example due to misconfigured authorisation or resource configuration problems
- If the function blows up without returning a proper response
- If the function returns a response that's not in the exact format that API Gateway expects

The *Resources* screen in the API Gateway Web Console is super useful for troubleshooting integration problems. When you get a 403 response and it's baffling you, navigate to the web console page for the API Gateway resource and click the *Test* link in the *Client* box (see the left side of Figure 6.2). A diagnostic test screen will open. You can enter request information, such as query strings and headers, then click the blue *Test* button towards the bottom of the screen. API Gateway will call the Lambda function simulating the HTTP request and then print out a bunch of diagnostic information, including all data sent to the back end and received back (Figure 6.4). This will help you discover the real problem and find out how to fix it.

Figure 6.4: *API Gateway testing prints out detailed diagnostic information.*

Processing request parameters

Let's now add a handler to deal with the form submissions. We did not set a specific form action URL, but we did set the form method to POST. When the form is submitted, this will make browsers send the information to the same URL where the form was displayed, but using the HTTP POST method. We can use the method to differentiate between the actions. If the Lambda function receives a GET call, it can show the form. If it receives a POST, it can process the submission.

In Chapter 4, we added some simple event logging into the sample function. Open the CloudWatch log and look at one of those events. You'll see that the method is in the httpMethod field of the event (Figure 6.5).

Figure 6.5: *The httpMethod field in an API Gateway Lambda Proxy event contains the HTTP method of the request.*

We can now simply set up a simple static response thanking the users for submitting the form. The function just needs to check for the httpMethod and decide what to send back.

——————————————————— ch6/hello-world/app.js ———————————————————

```
1   const htmlResponse = require('./html-response');
2   const formHtml = `
3     <html>
4     <head>
5       <meta charset="utf-8"/>
6     </head>
7     <body>
8       <form method="POST">
9         Please enter your name:
10        <input type="text" name="name"/>
11        <br/>
12        <input type="submit" />
13      </form>
14    </body>
15    </html>
16  `;
17
18  const thanksHtml = `
19    <html>
20    <head>
21      <meta charset="utf-8"/>
22    </head>
23    <body>
24      <h1>Thanks</h1>
25      <p>We received your submission</p>
26    </body>
27    </html>
28  `;
29
30  exports.lambdaHandler = async (event, context) => {
31    console.log(JSON.stringify(event, null, 2));
32
33    if (event.httpMethod === 'GET') {
34      return htmlResponse(formHtml);
35    } else {
36      return htmlResponse(thanksHtml);
37    }
38  };
```

In order for API Gateway to pass through POST requests as well, we need to add an additional event. In the template, copy the existing HelloWorld event and save it under a new name. Also change its method to post. (You'll need to add lines 24-28 from the following listing.)

—————————————————— ch6/template.yaml ——————————————————

```
  HelloWorldFunction:
    Type: AWS::Serverless::Function
    Properties:
      CodeUri: hello-world/
      Handler: app.lambdaHandler
      Runtime: nodejs12.x
      AutoPublishAlias: live
      Events:
        HelloWorld:
          Type: Api
          Properties:
            Path: /hello
            Method: get
        SubmitForm:
          Type: Api
          Properties:
            Path: /hello
            Method: post
```

Now build, package and deploy the stack. Open the API URL in a browser, submit a form, and you should see a 'thank you' message (Figure 6.6).

Figure 6.6: *The POST handler is now responding to our requests.*

SAM hides most of the complexity of setting up an API Gateway and linking it with a Lambda function. It does, still, allow you to configure the API for advanced use cases. For some common settings, you can influence how SAM creates the implicit API Gateway by modifying the Globals section of the template. For more advanced settings, we need to tell SAM to skip implicitly creating an API and to use an API we configure ourselves.

> ## ANY method
>
> API Gateway also supports a special marker value for HTTP methods, any, that matches all methods. We could have changed the original event to use any instead of introducing a new event here, but I wanted to show you how to add events.

As an example of configuring the implicit API with a global property, we'll change the deployment endpoint configuration to optimise for regional deployment in the next section. After that, as an example of how to take complete control and skip the implicit API, we'll change the /Prod part of the URL to something nicer.

Using global settings to configure the implicit API

With the Lambda Proxy integration, API Gateway just packages all the request properties and forwards them to Lambda. However, if you look at one of the request logs carefully (Figure 6.5), you'll notice some headers that do not look like they are coming from a browser. For example, CloudFront-Viewer-Country shows the ISO country code where the request originated. This is because the request did not go directly from a browser to API Gateway. Instead, it first went to the AWS global content distribution system called CloudFront, which put in some additional headers.

SAM can set up two types of API Gateway configuration: edge-optimised and regional.

Edge optimised APIs are served from a specific region, but the clients connect to the nearest AWS presence point. So far, we've been deploying an API to the us-east-1 region in North Virginia, USA. With edge-optimised APIs, a user from Germany will likely connect first to an AWS CloudFront endpoint in Frankfurt, then the request will pass to the API through the internal AWS links, not through the public internet. AWS has fast links between regions, and using the nearest point of presence in general improves connection latency for global users. But this also means that someone trying to access the API from North Virginia will go through an unnecessary intermediary.

Regional APIs do not set up an intermediary connection using CloudFront. If we deployed a regional API to us-east-1, a user from Germany would connect to the AWS endpoint in North Virginia through the public internet. That would likely make global connections worse, but local connections would be slightly faster.

Although CloudFront adds additional cost to each request, removing it may not actually reduce the overall price significantly. Both API Gateway and CloudFront charge for the number of requests and for data transfer. Data transfer through CloudFront is slightly cheaper than using API Gateway, and AWS does not charge for transfer between its own services. With both services in the pipeline, the requests are slightly more expensive, but data transfers are slightly cheaper. In conclusion, don't deploy regional endpoints expecting to save money, but do it if you want to remove an intermediary for connections in a specific territory.

By default, SAM assumes that you want to take advantage of edge-optimised APIs, so your users globally get faster responses if you deploy it to just one region. If you plan to deploy entire stacks in different AWS regions, so you can serve users locally, tell SAM to use regional APIs.

To change the endpoint type of the API that SAM creates automatically, create an `Api` property in the `Globals` section. Then add a sub-property called `EndpointConfiguration` inside, and set it to `REGIONAL` (add lines 10-11 from the following listing to your template).

───────────────────────── ch6/template-regional.yaml ─────────────────────────

```
 7   Globals:
 8     Function:
 9       Timeout: 3
10     Api:
11       EndpointConfiguration: REGIONAL
```

Build, package and deploy the stack again then trigger another request and look at the logs. CloudFront headers should no longer appear, because the API is now regional (Figure 6.7).

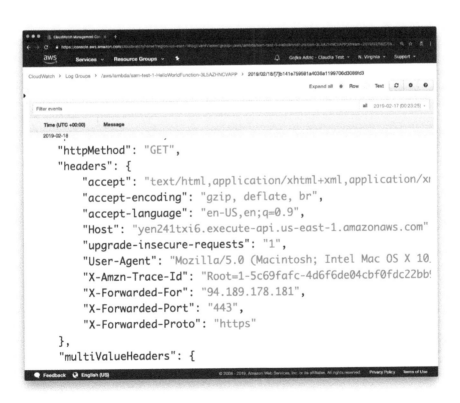

Figure 6.7: *Regional APIs do not pass through the content distribution network, so there are no more CloudFront headers.*

For a full list of properties you can configure this way, check out the Globals Section[1] documentation page for AWS SAM.

Building a different template

Notice that the title of the previous listing has a different template file name (`template-regional.yaml`). If you are following the tutorial, just modify your main template file with the proposed change. If you want to use the source code package from https://runningserverless.com, you'll find several templates in the directory for this chapter – one with the regional configuration and one without. So far, we've always used `sam build` to prepare the default `template.yaml` file for packaging. You can use the `-t <FILE NAME>` option to tell SAM to use a specific template file. To build directly from the regional template example, use the following command:

```
sam build -t template-regional.yaml
```

The commands to package and deploy stay the same as before.

Creating parameterised CloudFormation stacks

In the stack template, we configured events for the `/hello-world` path. But the actual path in the API is slightly different, and it includes the `/Prod/` prefix. This is because SAM automatically creates a `Prod` stage for the implicit API.

In the API Gateway terminology, a *stage* is a published version of the API configuration. Using stages allows API Gateway to serve a stable version of the API while users are adding or configuring resources to prepare for a new version. In the context of API Gateway, stages serve a very similar purpose to aliases of Lambda functions. You can even set up a 'canary' deployment where one version of the API gets just a percentage of traffic for a deployed stage.

An API needs at least one stage so that it becomes publicly accessible. In theory, you can set up different stages for development, testing or production with a single API, but with SAM that's not convenient. It's a lot more common to create completely different stacks for different pipeline steps. The APIs you create using SAM will usually have a single stage.

The standard stage name, `Prod`, forces users to remember a mix of upper-case and lower-case letters. I don't particularly like having mixed-case URLs; they are a lot more error prone than if everything is just lower case. SAM lets you configure the stage name for an API, but you can't set this through the `Globals` section. We'll have to create an API explicitly and configure it.

---

[1]https://github.com/awslabs/serverless-application-model/blob/master/docs/globals.rst

CloudFormation API or SAM API?

CloudFormation has two resources for managing Rest APIs, `AWS::ApiGateway::RestApi` and `AWS::ApiGatewayV2::Api`. SAM provides a convenient wrapper around lower-level resources with `AWS::Serverless::Api`. When you use the SAM wrapper, you don't need to set up security policies for Lambda event mappings and worry about connecting to the right Lambda version or alias. To achieve the same result with lower-level resources, you would need a lot more template code.

You can use the reference to a SAM wrapper resource instead of lower-level resources in all the places where CloudFormation expects the identifier of a REST API. If SAM created an API implicitly, you can get its identifier using the automatically generated `ServerlessRestApi` reference.

Defining stack parameters

I dislike having /Prod/ in the URL, but that's a matter of taste. Whatever I choose as a nice URL, other people might not like. We can make a template that works for everybody by introducing a *stack parameter*. Parameters are a way to create customisable stacks. Users can set the parameter value to provide their own configuration when deploying a stack. This makes it easy to publish reusable stacks and even connect the outputs of one stack to the inputs of another.

Let's first create a parameter to hold the stage name. Define a top-level section called `Parameters` in your template. For example, add it immediately after the `Globals` section. Set up a parameter by providing its name as a key then list the expected type and default value as in the following listing:

———————————————— ch6/template-custom-stage.yaml ————————————————

```
10  Parameters:
11    AppStage:
12      Type: String
13      Default: api
```

The default value setting is optional and just makes it slightly easier to deploy the stack without having to set all parameters. If you don't configure a default value for a parameter and don't provide a value during deployment, CloudFormation will refuse to set up the stack. For cases where you actually want the default to be undefined, use a blank string between quotes as the value (`Default: ''`).

Referencing parameter values

We can now create an API Gateway in the `Resources` section of the template. Add a new resource of type `AWS::Serverless::Api` (on the same indentation level as the `HelloWorldFunction`) and set up the `StageName` property. In the previous chapter, we used the `!Ref` function and turned a logical name of a CloudFormation resource into its physical name. The same function works on parameters. To use a parameter value directly in a YAML template, just put the parameter name after `!Ref`, as in the following listing:

───────────────── ch6/template-custom-stage.yaml ─────────────────

```
20   WebApi:
21     Type: AWS::Serverless::Api
22     Properties:
23       StageName: !Ref AppStage
```

The `AWS::Serverless::Api` resource allows you to quickly set up caching, canary deployments, authorisation and a lot more. For a full list of properties you can configure using this resource, check out the AWS::Serverless::Api resource page[2] in the SAM documentation.

The logical identifiers of resources (such as `WebApi` and `HelloWorldFunction`) are also references. This means that we can use `!Ref WebApi` in any place where CloudFormation expects an ID of an API Gateway. SAM events with the `Api` type have a third optional property, `RestApiId`, where we can specify a non-default API. Add this into both events of the template (lines 37 and 43 in the next code listing).

───────────────── ch6/template-custom-stage.yaml ─────────────────

```
24   HelloWorldFunction:
25     Type: AWS::Serverless::Function
26     Properties:
27       CodeUri: hello-world/
28       Handler: app.lambdaHandler
29       Runtime: nodejs12.x
30       AutoPublishAlias: live
31       Events:
32         HelloWorld:
33           Type: Api
34           Properties:
35             Path: /hello
36             Method: get
37             RestApiId: !Ref WebApi
38         SubmitForm:
39           Type: Api
40           Properties:
41             Path: /hello
42             Method: post
43             RestApiId: !Ref WebApi
```

Finally, we need to somehow discover the ID of the newly created API, so that we can use it to send requests. Let's change the value of the `HelloWorldApi` output in the template to use `WebApi` instead of the built-in `ServerlessRestApi`. While we're doing that, let's also change the hard-coded `Prod` stage to the `AppStage` parameter.

───────────────────────

[2]https://github.com/awslabs/serverless-application-model/blob/develop/versions/2016-10-31.md#awsserverlessapi

——————————— ch6/template-custom-stage.yaml ———————————

```
Outputs:
  HelloWorldApi:
    Description: "API Gateway endpoint URL"
    Value: !Sub "https://${WebApi}.execute-api.${AWS::Region}.amazonaws.com/${AppStage}/hello/"
```

!Ref or !Sub

Notice how we use references on line 47 of the previous listing. Instead of !Ref, we use !Sub. Because of an exclamation mark, this is again a function call. The Sub function substitutes references enclosed within ${} with related values. Use !Ref when you need the actual reference, and !Sub when you want to combine references with some other text, for example to construct a URL.

Build, package and deploy your stack, then list stack outputs or find your stack in the AWS Web Console. You'll see that the API endpoint has a different URL:

```
$ aws cloudformation describe-stacks --stack-name sam-test-1 --query Stacks[].Outputs
[
    [
        {
            "OutputKey": "HelloWorldApi",
            "OutputValue": "https://keqbc29e60.execute-api.us-east-1.amazonaws.com/api/hello/",
            "Description": "API Gateway endpoint URL"
        }
    ]
]
```

Notice that the path prefix is now api, because that was the default value for the AppStage parameter in the template. The domain name is different as well, because SAM created a new API Gateway for us. API Gateway domain names are based on their ID, so when we stopped using the implicit API and created our own, the API ID changed.

Custom API domain names

You can set up an API to work with your own domain name instead of a generic AWS URL. For example, create an API that responds to https://api.company.com. That is relatively straightforward to do from the API Gateway Web Console: select the *Custom Domain Names* option in the left menu and follow the instructions on the screen. For detailed instructions, check out the Set up Custom Domain Name for an API[3] page in the AWS API Gateway documentation.

---

[3]https://docs.aws.amazon.com/apigateway/latest/developerguide/how-to-custom-domains.html

Provide parameter values during deployment

If you don't like my choice for the stage name, you can modify it very easily. There is no need to build and package again. We use the same template and just redeploy it with different parameter values. Add the `--parameter-overrides` to the deployment command, and then put the parameter name and value separated by an equals sign. For example:

```
sam deploy --template-file output.yaml --stack-name sam-test-1 --capabilities CAPABILITY_IAM
↪    --parameter-overrides AppStage=test
```

List the stack outputs after the deployment, and you'll see that the stage is now called test:

```
1   $ aws cloudformation describe-stacks --stack-name=sam-test-1 --query Stacks[].Outputs
2   [
3     [
4       {
5         "OutputKey": "HelloWorldApi",
6         "OutputValue": "https://kdlawk4vtf.execute-api.us-east-1.amazonaws.com/test/hello/",
7         "Description": "API Gateway endpoint URL"
8       }
9     ]
10  ]
```

If you want to provide multiple parameters, just separate them with spaces. For example:

```
sam deploy --parameter-overrides AppStage=api AppName=Demo
```

Making stack parameters more user-friendly

Although we can specify an API stage now, there's nothing really preventing people from entering invalid stage names and breaking the stack completely. The Type field can catch some silly errors such as trying to provide text for a numerical value, but we used a `String` here, and almost anything is a valid string. Cloud-Formation doesn't know how we intended to use the parameter, so it can't know to validate it. This means that detecting problems can take a long time, especially with complex stacks. CloudFormation will likely start creating resources until it hits an invalid one, and then explode. For complex templates, especially when you use the same parameter in multiple places, error messages might not even make a lot of sense to an average user.

Luckily, there are several ways to make template parameters more user-friendly. We can explain the purpose of a parameter using the `Description` field and even set up automatic validation. With strings, we can set up `MinLength` and `MaxLength` properties to control the allowed size, and provide a regular expression to validate the contents using `AllowedPattern`. For numbers, we can configure the applicable range using `MinValue` and `MaxValue`. If the users should only be able to choose from a pre-determined set of options, we can use `AllowedValues` and provide a list. To help people understand potential validation errors more easily, explain the limits using `ConstraintDescription`.

Here is how we could potentially set up the stage values to only accept one to 10 letters:

──────────────────── ch6/template-custom-stage.yaml ────────────────────

```
Parameters:
  AppStage:
    Type: String
    Default: api
    Description: API Gateway stage, used as a prefix for the endpoint URLs
    AllowedPattern: ^[A-Za-z]+$
    MaxLength: 10
    MinLength: 1
    ConstraintDescription: "1-10 Latin letters"
```

Build, package and deploy this stack now, but try providing a stage name with a number during deployment. CloudFormation should complain quickly and show you a nice message about how to fix the problem:

```
$ sam deploy --template-file output.yaml --stack-name sam-test-1 --capabilities CAPABILITY_IAM
  --parameter-overrides AppStage=12345

An error occurred (ValidationError) when calling the CreateChangeSet operation: Parameter AppStage
  failed to satisfy constraint: 1-10 Latin letters
```

Check out the CloudFormation Parameters[4] documentation page for more information on validation settings.

Interesting experiments

- Break the Lambda function for showing the HTML form, so it blows up during processing. See how API Gateway handles that kind of situation and check whether you can find the error in the Cloud-Watch logs.
- Try wrapping the error into a try/catch block that will return a valid HTTP response explaining the error. For example, use HTTP code 500, reserved for internal server errors. (Hint: you'll have to modify html-response.js to accept a custom status code.) See how the error report differs from the one when the function just blows up.
- Try implementing an HTTP redirect from a Lambda function (hint: use code 302 and put a destination URL into the Location header), and then navigate to the API URL from a browser to see the redirect in action.

─────────────────────

[4]https://docs.aws.amazon.com/AWSCloudFormation/latest/UserGuide/parameters-section-structure.html

7. Using external storage

This chapter explains how to connect a Lambda function to persistent storage such as a file system or a database. You'll also learn about passing configuration to Lambda functions, and dealing with resource access permissions.

The application we deployed in the previous chapter is stateless. It thanks the user for submitting a form, but we are not really preserving that data anywhere. Users won't really like just being ignored.

Lambda instances have a local file system you can write to, connected to the system's temporary path. Anything stored there is only accessible to that particular container, and it will be lost once the instance is stopped. This might be useful for temporarily caching results, but not for persistent storage. We'll need to move the user data outside the container.

Cloud storage options

There are three main choices for persistent storage in the cloud:

- Network file systems
- Relational databases
- Key-value stores

Network file systems are generally not a good choice for Lambda functions, for two reasons. The first is that attaching an external file system volume takes a significant amount of time. Anything that slows down initialisation is a big issue with automatic scaling, because it can amplify problems with cold starts and request latency. The second issue is that very few network storage systems can cope with potentially thousands of concurrent users, so we'd have to severely limit concurrency for Lambda functions to use network file systems without overloading them. The most popular external file storage on AWS is the Elastic Block Store (EBS), which could not even be attached to Lambda functions at the time when I wrote this.

Relational databases are good when you need to store data for flexible queries, but you pay for that flexibility with higher operational costs. Most relational database types are designed for persistent connections and introduce an initial handshake between the database service and user code to establish a connection. This initialisation can create problems with latency and cold starts, similar to what happens with network file systems. Since December 2019, AWS offer a service called RDS Proxy[1] that somewhat reduces the problem of database connection initialisations (think of it as a managed external database connection pool). However, at the time when I wrote this, the service was still offered only as a preview, and available in a small minority of AWS regions.

In general with relational databases you have to plan for capacity and reserve it up front, which is completely opposite to request-based pricing for Lambda functions. Increasing capacity usually involves data migration to a different storage, or stopping and restarting database server clusters. Both those operations are too slow to track auto-scaling Lambda functions. AWS now offers some relational databases on a pay-per-connection basis (for example AWS Aurora Serverless[2]), but supporting a very high number of concurrent requests usually requires a lot of processing power, so relational databases get quite expensive.

This leaves key-value stores as the most frequent choice for persistence for Lambda functions. Key-value stores are generally optimised for writing and retrieving objects by a primary key, not for ad-hoc queries

---

[1]https://aws.amazon.com/blogs/compute/using-amazon-rds-proxy-with-aws-lambda/
[2]https://aws.amazon.com/rds/aurora/serverless/

on groups of objects. Because the data is segmented, not interlinked, key-value stores are a lot less computationally demanding than relational databases, and their work can be parallelised and scaled much more easily. AWS offers several types of key-value store that work well with Lambda.

The two major choices in this category are Simple Storage Service (S3) and DynamoDB. Both require no initialisation handshakes to establish a connection, they can scale on demand, so Lambda spikes will not overload them, and AWS charges actual utilisation for them, priced per request. Actually, users can choose whether they want to pay for DynamoDB based on reserved capacity or on demand. Even in reserved capacity mode it's relatively easy to add or remove writer or reader units according to short-term traffic patterns, so you don't have to worry about running out of capacity.

Keeping the HTTPS connection alive

Although DynamoDB and S3 do not have application hand-shake overhead, Lambda talks to them using HTTPS, which has a protocol-level initialisation overhead. If your function performs several operations on the same storage in quick succession, you can speed up work by reusing the HTTPS connections. The way to achieve this depends on the programming language and client library you use to connect to AWS services, but it usually involves setting the 'Keep Alive' flag when using the AWS SDK. For Node.js, you can enable this feature by setting the AWS_NODEJS_CONNECTION_REUSE_ENABLED environment variable to 1.

S3 is an *object store*, designed for large binary unstructured data. It can store individual objects up to 5 TB. The objects are aggregated into *buckets*. A bucket is like a namespace or a database table, or, if you prefer a file system analogy, it is like a disk drive. Buckets are always located in a particular region. You can easily set up *cross-region replication*[3] for faster local access or backups. However, generally it's best if one region is the reference data source, because multi-master replication with S3 is not easy to set up.

DynamoDB is a *document database*, or, if you like buzzwords, a NoSQL database. Although it can keep binary objects as well, it's really designed for storing structured textual (JSON) data, supporting individual items up to 400 KB. DynamoDB stores items in *tables*, which can either be in a particular region or globally replicated. DynamoDB Global Tables[4] supports multi-master replication, so clients can write into the same table or even the same item from multiple regions at the same time, with local access latency.

S3 is designed for throughput, not necessarily predictable (or very low) latency. It can easily deal with bursts in traffic requests, especially if the requests are for different items.

DynamoDB is designed for low latency and sustained usage patterns. If the average item is relatively small, especially if items are less than 4KB, DynamoDB is significantly faster than S3 for individual operations. Although DynamoDB can scale on demand, it does not do that as quickly as S3. If there are sudden bursts of traffic, requests to DynamoDB may end up throttled for a while.

S3 operations generally work on entire items. Atomic batch operations on groups of objects are not possible, and it's difficult to work with parts of an individual object. There are some exceptions to this, such as retrieving byte ranges from an object, but appending content to a single item from multiple sources concurrently is not easy.

---

[3]https://docs.aws.amazon.com/AmazonS3/latest/dev/crr.html
[4]https://aws.amazon.com/dynamodb/global-tables/

DynamoDB works with structured documents, so its smallest atom of operation is a property inside an item. You can, of course, store binary unstructured information to DynamoDB, but that's not really the key use case. For structured documents, multiple writers can concurrently modify properties of the same item, or even append to the same array. DynamoDB can efficiently handle batch operations and conditional updates, even atomic transactions on multiple items.

S3 is more useful for extract-transform-load data warehouse scenarios than for ad-hoc or online queries. There are services that allow querying structured data within S3, for example AWS Athena,[5] but this is slow compared to DynamoDB and relational databases. DynamoDB understands the content of its items, and you can set up indexes for efficiently querying properties of items.

Both DynamoDB and S3 are designed for parallel work and shards (blocks of storage assigned to different processors), so they need to make allowances for consistency. S3 provides eventual consistency. With DynamoDB you can optionally enforce strong read consistency. This means that DynamoDB is better if you need to ensure that two different processes always get exactly the same information while a record is being updated.

S3 can pretend to be a web server and let end user devices access objects directly using HTTPS. Accessing data inside Dynamo requires AWS SDK with IAM authorisation.

S3 supports automatic versioning, so it's trivially easy to track a history of changes or even revert an object to a previous state. Dynamo does not provide object versioning out of the box. You can implement it manually, but it's difficult to block the modification of old versions.

Although the pricing models are different enough that there is no straight comparison, with all other things equal DynamoDB ends up being significantly cheaper for working with small items. On the other hand, S3 has several ways of cheaply archiving infrequently used objects. DynamoDB does not have multiple storage classes.

As a general rule of thumb, if you want to store potentially huge objects and only need to process individual objects at a time, choose S3. If you need to store small bits of structured data, with minimal latency, and potentially need to process groups of objects in atomic transactions, choose DynamoDB.

Both systems have workarounds for operations that are not as efficient as they would be in the other system. You can chunk large objects into DynamoDB items, and you can likewise set up a text search engine for large documents stored on S3. But some operations are significantly less hassle with one system than with another.

The nice aspect of both DynamoDB and S3 is that you do not have to predict capacity or pay for installation fees. There is no upfront investment that you then need to justify by putting all your data into the same place, so you can mix both systems and use them for different types of information. Look at the different usage patterns for different blocks of data then choose between Dynamo or S3 for each individual data type.

At MindMup, for example, we use S3 to store user files and most user requests, such as share invitations and conversion requests. We never need to run ad-hoc queries on those objects or process them in groups. We always access them by primary key, one at a time. We use DynamoDB to store account information, such as subscription data and payment references, because we often query this data based on attributes and want to sometimes process groups of related accounts together.

---

[5]https://aws.amazon.com/athena/

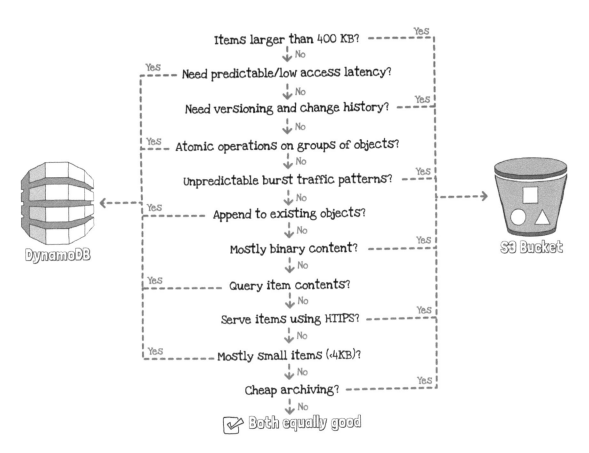

Figure 7.1: *Typical usage patterns for S3 and DynamoDB*

Still need a relational database?

If you really need to get data coming from users into a relational database or a network file system from Lambda, it's often better to create two functions. One can be user-facing, outside a VPC, so that it can start quickly, write to a document database or a transient external storage (such a queue), and respond to users quickly. The other function can move the data from the document database to the relational storage. You can put another service between the two functions, such as SQS or Kinesis, to buffer and constrain parallel migration work, so that you don't overload the downstream systems and that the processing does not suffer as much from cold starts.

In order to store data submitted by users with web forms, we don't necessarily need to ensure very low latency. Users will be submitting information over HTTPS connections anyway, so they won't notice a few dozen milliseconds more. On the other hand, we may want to collect large attachments at potentially unpredictable traffic spike intervals, so working with S3 will be easier.

Let's modify our application to save submitted forms to S3 before thanking the users. First, we'll need an S3 bucket so we can save information to it.

We could create an S3 bucket outside the SAM template and then pass its name to SAM as a parameter, similarly to how we made the API stage name configurable in Chapter 6. This is a good option if you want the stack to connect to some pre-existing resource, for example to integrate with a third-party service. In this case, we don't care too much about backwards compatibility with pre-existing resources, so it's easier to just create the bucket directly in the stack. In the resources section, for example just below the `Resources` header, add an entry of type `AWS::S3::Bucket` and give it some meaningful name, for example `UploadS3Bucket`. Put it on the same indentation level as the other resources, such as the old `WebApi`:

─────────────────────── ch7/template.yaml ───────────────────────

```
15  UploadS3Bucket:
16    Type: AWS::S3::Bucket
```

Lambda access rights

AWS does not trust a Lambda function to access a database or an S3 bucket just because they belong to the same account. You need to explicitly allow the use of each external resource from a Lambda function. To do that, we'll need to modify the IAM policy associated with a function.

Our function currently has two actions: displaying a form and processing it. The form processing action will need access to an S3 bucket, but the form display action does not need any specific security access. When two different actions need different security levels, it's usually a good time to start thinking about breaking them into different Lambda functions.

With container-based applications, an API server process usually needs a superset of all the security permissions for all the contained actions. That makes setup and deployment easier, but it also means that a small security bug can easily turn into a disaster. If intruders break through a gatekeeper process, they can easily access all back-end resources. With Lambda functions, separating actions according to their security needs becomes very easy. Each function can have specific access to only the necessary resources. If a third-party dependency introduces a security issue in one of our API endpoints, the keys to the kingdom are still locked in a safe.

In Chapter 6 we created a new API endpoint to handle POST requests and just wired it up to the same function as the GET handler. Let's split two endpoints into two functions so we can manage security better (Figure 7.2).

We can use this opportunity for some nice housekeeping:

1. Rename the old Lambda function from HelloWorld to ShowFormFunction, so its purpose becomes clearer.
2. Rename the function code directory on your disk from hello-world to something more meaningful, such as user-form, and update the CodeUri property of the function accordingly.
3. Rename app.js inside the project code directory to something more meaningful, for example show-form.js, and update the Handler property of the function accordingly.
4. Rename the first event mapping to something meaningful, for example ShowForm.
5. Finally, instead of /hello as the API resource path, just use the root resource (/).

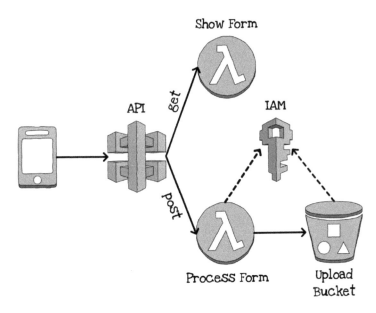

Figure 7.2: *We'll divide processing into two functions to control security better.*

We'll move the second event handler into a new Lambda function, so you can delete it from this block. The remaining configuration for the first function should look like in the following listing:

—————————————————— ch7/template.yaml ——————————————————

```
21  ShowFormFunction:
22    Type: AWS::Serverless::Function
23    Properties:
24      CodeUri: user-form/
25      Handler: show-form.lambdaHandler
26      Runtime: nodejs12.x
27      Events:
28        ShowForm:
29          Type: Api
30          Properties:
31            Path: /
32            Method: get
33            RestApiId: !Ref WebApi
```

We can also change the source code for the form display Lambda function. It no longer needs to handle post requests, so we can make it simpler. Update it to look like in the following listing:

—————————————————— ch7/user-form/show-form.js ——————————————————

```
1   const htmlResponse = require('./html-response');
2   const formHtml = `
3     <html>
4     <head>
5       <meta charset="utf-8"/>
6     </head>
7     <body>
8       <form method="POST">
9         Please enter your name:
10        <input type="text" name="name"/>
11        <br/>
12        <input type="submit" />
13      </form>
14    </body>
15    </html>
16  `;
17  exports.lambdaHandler = async (event, context) => {
18    return htmlResponse(formHtml);
19  };
```

The start of the second function configuration will be very similar to the first one, apart from the HTTP method and the JavaScript file reference. Let's make it talk to process-form.js, which we'll create in a minute, and use the POST method. Add a block similar to the code in the next listing:

──────────────── ch7/template.yaml ────────────────

```
ProcessFormFunction:
  Type: AWS::Serverless::Function
  Properties:
    CodeUri: user-form/
    Handler: process-form.lambdaHandler
    Runtime: nodejs12.x
    Events:
      SubmitForm:
        Type: Api
        Properties:
          Path: /
          Method: post
          RestApiId: !Ref WebApi
```

Generating unique references

Before we start working on the second function, there's an important technical aspect of working with S3 that we need to consider, which will also come into play frequently when using other storage systems. S3 isn't really an atomic database; it's eventually consistent. That means it's not safe to check whether a file name exists and, if not, then upload something there. We need some way of creating unique references to avoid naming conflicts. A typical solution for this would be to use some kind of unique ID generator, but then we have a problem with traceability. It's not easy to correlate logs and traces with outputs.

Each Lambda request has a unique request ID, which is automatically printed into the logs. You can read it from the second argument of the Lambda function, using context.awsRequestId. This is a great candidate for unique file names or message identifiers created from a Lambda function. Using a reference based on the request ID makes it unique but also easy to correlate with a processing session. Even more importantly, if the Lambda runtime retries processing an event after an error, it will use the same request ID. So if the function dies half-way through working and Lambda spins up another container to recover from the error, it won't generate two different files.

Using AWS resources from Lambda functions

We can use the AWS SDK in the Lambda function to talk to other AWS resources, including S3. Normally, when using the AWS SDK, we need to provide authentication details when instantiating the API. When using the AWS SDK inside a Lambda function, just instantiate the service objects without providing credentials, like in the following listing:

—————————————————— ch7/user-form/process-form.js ——————————————————

```
2  const aws = require('aws-sdk');
3  const s3 = new aws.S3();
```

Lambda functions run under temporary access credentials, valid only for a few minutes, and they are already set up in the environment by the time your function starts. AWS SDK functions will pick that up automatically.

We can now use the standard S3 SDK method putObject to send data to a bucket. This requires at least three parameters:

- Body should contain the contents of the object we're uploading. This could be a binary buffer or a string. In this case, we can just serialise the whole request to a string using JSON.stringify.
- Bucket should be the name of the target bucket. In the SAM template, we passed the bucket name to the Lambda function using an environment variable, so we can use process.env to read it.
- Key is the target file identifier on S3. We should make it unique to avoid conflicts.

Using third-party libraries in Lambda code

AWS SDK for JavaScript is already installed in a running Lambda environment, so we do not need to specifically add it as a dependency. The command sam build bundles dependencies with a function, so if you need to use any other third-party libraries, just install them to the project using NPM.

We could, of course, also install the AWS SDK. This would ensure that sam build packages a particular version, but it would also increase the size of the function package. The deployment process would become slightly slower, which would become noticeable for very simple functions such as the ones we're deploying. On the other hand, bundling AWS SDK with a function makes it easy to guarantee that the same version used for development and testing is also used in production. I like fixing the version for serious work, and use the provided library for quick experiments.

SAM does not package development dependencies, so if you want to use a third-party library just for testing, install it in your Node project with the -D flag (development-only flag).

When using JavaScript (not other languages), we need to convert the result of an AWS SDK call to a Promise object, to ensure that Lambda waits for the external call to finish before continuing. All SDK functions have a method, .promise(), that converts the callback-based invocation into a Promise object. To save the whole event payload to S3, we'll need to use code similar to the following listing:

———————————————— ch7/user-form/process-form.js ————————————————

```
7   await s3.putObject({
8     Bucket: bucketName,
9     Key: context.awsRequestId,
0     Body: JSON.stringify(event)
1   }).promise();
```

Don't forget a promise

With Node.js, Lambda functions must be async or return a Promise object. If you forget to convert an SDK call into a promise and wait for it to finish, the function will exit too soon and Lambda will kill the container before the network call completes. This does not apply to other runtimes (but you may need to synchronise with network requests differently).

Passing resource references to functions

In order to complete the function, we'll need, somehow, to tell it which bucket to use (line 8 in the previous listing). Lambda functions don't really know about SAM and CloudFormation resources, so the function can't just ask for the UploadS3Bucket resource. SAM will create the bucket using a randomised name, and we need to tell the Lambda function about the actual value.

We definitely don't want to hard code a bucket name in the function source, because then SAM can't automatically manage buckets. We could change the API Gateway resource to stick that information onto the request while it's passing through the API, for example as an additional header, but that requires messy request transformations. For situations such as this one, it's best to set a Lambda environment variable.

Environment variables are textual key-value pairs assigned to a running process. With a Node.js Lambda runtime, we can read them using the standard Node process.env object. SAM lets us configure those values in the template, so it's easy to pass the actual bucket name to a function based on the logical bucket reference.

Environment variables are great for configuring Lambda functions with references to other resources in the same SAM template. For more complex configuration scenarios, such as rotating secrets and reconfiguring services without redeployment, check out the AWS Systems Manager Parameter Store[6] and AWS Secrets Manager[7].

I tend to use all uppercase letters for environment variable names to clearly differentiate them from other values, but you can use any naming convention you like. Update the process-form.js file to look like in the following listing:

---

[6]https://docs.aws.amazon.com/systems-manager/latest/userguide/systems-manager-paramstore.html
[7]https://aws.amazon.com/secrets-manager/

---

ch7/user-form/process-form.js ────────

```
1   const htmlResponse = require('./html-response');
2   const aws = require('aws-sdk');
3   const s3 = new aws.S3();
4
5   exports.lambdaHandler = async (event, context) => {
6     const bucketName = process.env.UPLOAD_S3_BUCKET;
7     await s3.putObject({
8       Bucket: bucketName,
9       Key: context.awsRequestId,
10      Body: JSON.stringify(event)
11    }).promise();
12    const thanksHtml = `
13      <html>
14      <head>
15        <meta charset="utf-8"/>
16      </head>
17      <body>
18        <h1>Thanks</h1>
19        <p>We received your submission</p>
20        <p>Reference: ${context.awsRequestId}</p>
21        </p>
22      </body>
23      </html>
24      `;
25
26    return htmlResponse(thanksHtml);
27  };
```

SAM can configure environment variables for a function using the Environment property. It must have a Variables sub-property, which can then contain a map of keys and values. We can use the !Ref function to convert the logical name of a CloudFormation resource into its physical ID. Add the following three lines to the ProcessFormFunction template, at the same indentation level as other function properties (so Environment should be aligned with Events):

---

ch7/template.yaml ────────

```
47  Environment:
48    Variables:
49      UPLOAD_S3_BUCKET: !Ref UploadS3Bucket
```

Authorising access with IAM policies

Passing a reference to the bucket in an environment variable will let the Lambda function know where to write, but it still won't have the permission to do that. We need to configure IAM to allow storage access. SAM hides that complexity significantly and avoids dozens of lines of boilerplate code for each function. It has convenient policy templates for popular AWS services, including S3. In this case we can use the S3FullAccessPolicy, which gives a Lambda function read and write access to all objects in a bucket.

In the ProcessFormFunction template, specify a Policies property, followed by list of policies. (Note that YAML uses dashes to create lists, so you'll need to use a dash prefix before each element in the Policy list.) This section should be at the same indentation level as the other function properties, so Policies should be aligned with Events and Environment:

———————————————————— ch7/template.yaml ————————————————————

```
Policies:
  - S3FullAccessPolicy:
      BucketName: !Ref UploadS3Bucket
```

Here are some other interesting policy templates from SAM:

- S3ReadPolicy provides read-only access to a bucket.
- LambdaInvokePolicy allows calling a specific Lambda function.
- DynamoDBCrudPolicy provides full access to a DynamoDB table.

SAM developers are frequently adding policy templates, so for an up-to-date list it's best to check the SAM GitHub repository. You can find the list of all supported templates and their arguments in the all_policy_templates.yaml[8] file.

SAM policies or CloudFormation policies

SAM policy templates are convenient, but relatively crude. You can create much finer-grained policies directly with IAM, for example to grant access only to specific attributes in the DynamoDB table, or only to files with specific prefixes on S3, and only for certain operations.
You can specify a full IAM policy in the SAM function Policies property, so you can mix and match templated and non-templated policies.

Technically, policies are not really assigned to a Lambda function. They are assigned to an IAM security role, which is associated with a Lambda function. SAM automatically creates a role for each function, named

---

[8]https://github.com/awslabs/serverless-application-model/blob/master/tests/translator/input/all_policy_templates.yaml

by appending the word Role to the function name. For example, for ShowFormFunction, the role resource will be called ShowFormFunctionRole. You can use that resource in any other CloudFormation IAM template, to configure the role in the ways that SAM can't do out of the box. See *CloudFormation Resources Generated By SAM*[9] for more information. If you want to manage the function roles explicitly, for example to set up a single shared role for several functions, use the Role property of a function and provide the role name or ARN. SAM will not create an implicit role for your function in this case.

We're almost ready to deploy this template with two different functions. Before we do that, remember that we changed the API Gateway resource path from /hello to just the root. Let's update the stack outputs accordingly, so we can get the new URL easily. Remove the word hello from the end of the URL in the stack outputs, and perhaps rename the HelloWorldApi output to something more meaningful.

────────────────────────────── ch7/template.yaml ──────────────────────────────

```
53  Outputs:
54    UserFormApi:
55      Description: "API Gateway endpoint URL"
56      Value: !Sub "https://${WebApi}.execute-api.${AWS::Region}.amazonaws.com/${AppStage}/"
```

In order to test whether our function is saving files to S3 correctly, we'll also need to know the name of the bucket that SAM created for us. So let's set up another template output so we can get that information easily. Add it at the same indentation level as UserFormApi.

────────────────────────────── ch7/template.yaml ──────────────────────────────

```
57  UploadBucket:
58    Description: "S3 Bucket for user information"
59    Value: !Ref UploadS3Bucket
```

Build, package and deploy the project again. This might take slightly longer than usual, because SAM needs to create two new functions and associated objects, remove the old functions and roles, and also create the bucket. Check out the stack outputs, and you should see the new URL (without /hello) and the bucket SAM created for us.

```
1   $ aws cloudformation describe-stacks --stack-name sam-test-1 --query Stacks[].Outputs
2   [
3     [
4       {
5         "OutputKey": "UserFormApi",
6         "OutputValue": "https://keqbc29e60.execute-api.us-east-1.amazonaws.com/api/",
7         "Description": "API Gateway endpoint URL"
8       },
9       {
10        "OutputKey": "UploadBucket",
11        "OutputValue": "sam-test-1-uploads3bucket-g6evg49hxobz",
12        "Description": "S3 Bucket for user information"
13      }
```

---

[9]https://github.com/awslabs/serverless-application-model/blob/master/docs/internals/generated_resources.rst

```
4    ]
5  ]
```

Open the application page in a browser and try it out. Once you submit the form, you should see a reference on the thank-you screen (Figure 7.3). The Lambda function will also store the full request body to S3, so you can process it later. Note that in this case we store the full request, not just the form data.

Figure 7.3: *The form processing Lambda function saved the file to S3 and provided the user with a reference.*

Open the AWS S3 Web Console, look for the bucket created by CloudFormation, and check out the contents. You should see a single file, named after the reference that the form handler page printed out.

Dealing with network timeouts

In this example, we're uploading relatively small files to S3, so that operation completes quickly. By default, Lambda allows a function just three seconds to finish. A process that is any longer will cause a timeout. If you plan to process larger blocks of data or perform many network requests within the same function, three seconds won't be enough.

You can increase the allowed time by setting the Timeout property in the function SAM template. This value is the number of seconds, and the maximum you can set it to is 900 (15 minutes). To change the value of the Timeout property for all functions in a template file, modify the Globals section.

When a Lambda function is talking to AWS resources, you generally don't need to worry too much about availability and local access latency. When a function is communicating with third-party services, don't ignore potential network problems. Increasing the timeout is good but does not really solve the problem. If a Lambda function times out, API Gateway will just return a generic error to the clients, and they won't know what happened. It's much better to set up a circuit breaker and interrupt a stalled network process while you still have time to respond with a sensible error message to your clients.

The Lambda context object, which we used to retrieve a unique request ID, has a few additional interesting properties. One of them is the function getRemainingTimeInMillis(), which returns the number of milliseconds left for the execution of the current function. Use this information to schedule an event a few seconds before the end of the function when talking to potentially unreliable external services or performing long-running tasks in a Lambda function. You can then clean up and respond to the client before the external resource times out.

In fact, letting the Lambda run for longer might not make a lot of difference over half a minute for HTTP requests. API Gateway also has a timeout, and it will kill any requests lasting more than 29 seconds. There is no way to change this, but if you find yourself in a situation where that's a problem, you probably need to rethink the application architecture a bit. In the next chapter, we will look at some nice solutions for long-running processes.

Check timeouts for all involved services

When using multiple AWS services, remember that they might have different timeout settings, so you may need to configure all of them or work around their constraints. For example, API Gateway limits requests to 30 seconds, so setting a long timeout value for Lambda functions driven by API Gateway has no real effect.

Interesting experiments

- Change the form handler (process-form.js) to store only the submitted form data, not the entire request payload.
- Remove the access permissions for the second function so it no longer has the rights to write to the S3 bucket, and then redeploy the stack. Try changing the code so it provides a nice error in case of storage access problems.

8. Cheaper, faster, serverless

This chapter shows how to start shifting the core responsibilities of typical servers to the AWS platform, and how to benefit from serverless architectures to make your application faster and cheaper. You'll also learn about the options to let client devices directly use AWS resources on your behalf.

In the previous chapters, we deployed a simple application that is ready for millions of users if necessary, but doesn't cost anything if nobody is using it. AWS operates and monitors the application, so most of the 'ops' part of DevOps is effectively included in the price. This is quite a nice outcome for such little effort, mostly achieved because we didn't have to write infrastructural code. With Lambda, API Gateway and S3, all that infrastructural stuff comes out of the box.

Our application still looks very similar to a typical three-tier server setup. In such an architecture, an application server usually contains the business logic, but also plays two more roles. It works as a gatekeeper and a workflow orchestration system. The application server approves or rejects client requests, talks to back-end storage, schedules asynchronous processing and passes back results to client devices. For highly available and scalable web applications, the code running on a client device usually talks to the application server through a load-balancing proxy. Our API Gateway resources work pretty much like the load-balancing proxy. Our form processing Lambda function might not control a network socket, but it's very much a gatekeeper to the S3 storage.

Although the application is already relatively cheap and fast, we can make it faster and cheaper by taking away the traditional server roles from Lambda functions. Out of the three responsibilities of the traditional application server, only the business logic should stay in Lambda functions. In this chapter, we'll remove the gatekeeper role from Lambda functions. In Chapter 9, we'll look at how to remove the orchestration role.

The goal of extracting the gatekeeper role from Lambda functions is to remove an unnecessary intermediary between client devices and network resources, such as the S3 storage. The client devices can write directly to S3. This can be quite controversial for people used to three-tier architectures. It's easy to think about storage such as file repositories or databases as back-end resources that need protection from client devices. But with AWS, services such as DynamoDB or S3 are not really in the back end. They are available directly over the internet, to you, to your users, and to everyone else. S3 won't trust a request coming from a Lambda function any more than a request coming directly from a client device.

Having a Lambda function sitting between a user device and S3 is not really useful if it only performs authorisation. S3 can do that itself. There's no need to suffer through the additional latency of API proxying and Lambda execution. For large files, this can make a huge difference, both in terms of speed and in terms of processing costs.

AWS provides several ways of temporarily granting clients the right to do very specific operations:

- We could let clients use the AWS SDK directly, and set up IAM users for each client.
- We could set up templated IAM policies for groups of end users authenticated with Amazon Cognito[1], a managed service for user credentials.
- We could use a Lambda function to create temporary grants for clients, so they can access our AWS resources in a limited way.

The first option, using IAM directly, is great for internal applications, and with a small number of named users. Each user can get their own specific privileges and sign in to the client application with an IAM username and password, and the client application can directly use AWS SDK to access storage, databases or queues. Client devices can even invoke Lambda functions directly to perform business logic that you do not want to expose to client application code. Users can have multi-factor authentication devices for increased security.

---

[1]https://aws.amazon.com/cognito/

The big limit with IAM is that you can only create about 1000 users for an AWS account, and those users can't register directly for your application. An administrator would have to set up individual users. Of course, you could build a Lambda function that can create IAM users and manage policies, but that function would need full access to your IAM resources, and that's a huge security risk.

The second option, using Cognito, is great for publicly facing applications. Cognito is a managed service for user data. It stores usernames and passwords securely, optionally allowing users to sign up themselves or even sign in through federated authentication systems (for example a company single sign-on or using Google accounts). You can configure Cognito to automatically allow end users to have limited access to your AWS resources. For example, you could allow users to read files from an S3 bucket, optionally only those files with a prefix matching the account ID. Similarly, you could allow users to read or write only certain fields of a DynamoDB record matching their ID. IAM supports templates with Cognito identities, so you could achieve this with a single policy, without having to create and assign policies to individual users. Cognito can even manage user groups with separate security policies. For example, you could create groups for guests, authors and moderators, with different access privileges.

The third option, using a Lambda function to create temporary grants, is great for anonymous access. This method allows you to safely pass on temporary access rights with the account credentials to client devices. It does not require the creation of any kind of user records or up-front registration. Temporary grants are also good for situations when templated policies are too restrictive, for example with Cognito users where access isn't easy to segment under a prefix matching the user identifier.

In this chapter, we'll change the form processing application to let users upload files directly to S3. We'll use Lambda functions just to authorise the requests. Lambda functions will no longer work as gatekeepers. The client requests will go through fewer intermediaries, execute faster, and the whole application will be cheaper to operate (Figure 8.1).

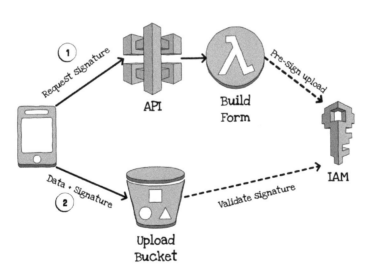

Figure 8.1: *Lambda functions will authorise access to S3, so client code can upload and read files directly.*

Signing requests

To explain how temporary grants work, I first need to explain the role of the security keys you entered when configuring command line access in Chapter 2. Each IAM user has two keys: an access key and a secret key. When the SDK makes a request to an AWS service, for example s3.putObject(), it sends the access key in the request headers. This allows the service to map the request to an AWS account. The SDK also sends a cryptographic signature based on the request body and the secret key, using Amazon's Signature Version 4 Signing Process[2] (SIGV4 algorithm). The receiving service uses the access key to locate the corresponding secret key in the IAM database, and also creates a SIGV4 signature for the request. If the two signatures match, AWS knows that the request was authorised by the user.

The interesting part of this is that some services accept templated signatures, so we can create a grant up front without knowing all the request parameters. This allows us to effectively produce temporary grants for users to perform limited operations with our AWS resources. For example, we could sign a request matching an S3 upload to a specific file key, in a specific bucket, up to a specific size, and only valid for a specific period of time. We can then safely send this signature to a client, without the risk of exposing the real secret key. The client code can try to upload a file and include the signature in the authorisation header. S3 will examine the signature, evaluate the request against the access policy, and allow or reject the request.

S3 will evaluate the signature both based on the restrictions in the temporary grant and the permissions assigned to the access key. The grant will be invalid if we sign the operation using a key that does not have access to the S3 bucket. This means that we can safely sign temporary grants from a Lambda function. A function can never pass on privileges that it does not itself have.

Using a Lambda function to just pre-sign uploads for client devices is very a common usage pattern. The AWS SDK for JavaScript already has a shortcut method for that operation, so you don't have to learn the details of the SIGV4 signature process. The method is s3.createPresignedPost. It takes a map of conditions such as the expiration time of the policy, partial or full matching on the uploaded file key, maximum allowed length and the default access level for the uploaded file. The function returns a list of fields that can be used to construct an HTML form.

There are two ways to use those fields. One is to create an HTML form directly and display it in a web page. Browsers will show a button to select a local file and post it to S3, and S3 will redirect to a specified page after a successful upload. Alternatively, we can use those fields to create a FormData browser object and upload the file using a background process, such as browser HTML5 fetch or XMLHttpRequest. The second approach is a lot more flexible, because we could use JavaScript to set the content type or target file name, and it would allow us to create a nicer user experience. But to keep things simple for now, we'll use the first approach and just let the browser show a form.

With a browser form workflow, we can tell S3 to redirect users somewhere after a successful upload. We can set up an API endpoint to handle the redirects, and then provide the URL to the function signing the credentials. The redirect comes from S3, not our API, so we'll need to define an absolute URL. We could pass the API ID and stage into a Lambda function as variables to create an absolute URL, but we don't have to. When API Gateway sends a request using the Lambda proxy integration, it will also add a requestContext

---

[2]https://docs.aws.amazon.com/general/latest/gr/signature-version-4.html

property with some operational information about the request itself. Check one of the CloudWatch logs from the previous deployments to see this. You'll see that it contains two interesting fields:

- `event.requestContext.domainName` is the full domain name used by the client to make the request.
- `event.requestContext.stage` is the API Gateway stage that received the request.

With API Gateway Lambda proxy integrations, the `requestContext` field contains all the contextual information about the API Gateway resource. This information does not come from the client devices, but from the API Gateway, so it's more reliable than using request headers.

Using the request context, we can easily construct an absolute URL to some other resource on the same API stage. For example, we'll set up a new function to confirm that the upload was successful on `/confirm`. To get the absolute URL, we need to use something like the code in the next listing:

――――――――――――――― ch8/user-form/show-form.js ―――――――――――――――

```
7  const apiHost = event.requestContext.domainName,
8    prefix = event.requestContext.stage,
9    redirectUrl = `https://${apiHost}/${prefix}/confirm`,
```

Instead of always returning a static web form, we'll create a pre-signed policy that allows users to upload a file. To prevent security problems, we'll constrain the uploads:

- We'll limit the upload key (file ID) to something based on the Lambda request ID. This ensures that one user can't overwrite a file uploaded by someone else.
- We'll limit the policy to just 10 minutes. This should be enough to upload even large files, but will not allow people to indefinitely reuse this same grant.
- We'll limit the size to just a few megabytes, so someone couldn't abuse the upload policy to overload our service and spend a lot of money for storage.
- We'll limit the access level to `private`, meaning that the file will only be accessible from our account. This prevents anyone abusing our system for public sharing.

――――――――――――――― ch8/user-form/show-form.js ―――――――――――――――

```
10  params = {
11    Bucket: process.env.UPLOAD_S3_BUCKET,
12    Expires: 600,
13    Conditions: [
14      ['content-length-range', 1, uploadLimitInMB * 1000000],
15    ],
16    Fields: {
17      success_action_redirect: redirectUrl,
18      acl: 'private',
19      key: context.awsRequestId + '.jpg'
20    }
21  },
22  form = s3.createPresignedPost(params);
```

Note that the key parameter on line 19 in the previous listing doesn't stop someone from uploading a file with the wrong content type. It just ensures a user can upload only to a very specific key. By using the AWS request ID, unique across all requests, we guarantee that multiple users do not overwrite each others uploads.

With the S3 form signing function, you can set many more constraints to ensure that direct uploads are safe enough for your context. For more information on all the available options, check out the S3 documentation page *Creating an HTML Form (Using AWS Signature Version 4)*[3].

Once we have a pre-signed policy, we will need to format it as an HTML form. To make the code easier to read, let's extract that responsibility into a separate method. Here is a utility function that will format the results of s3.createPresignedPost:

──────────────── ch8/user-form/build-form.js ────────────────

```
1   module.exports = function buildForm(form) {
2     const fieldNames = Object.keys(form.fields);
3     const fields = fieldNames.map(field =>
4       `<input type="hidden" name="${field}" value="${form.fields[field]}"/>`
5     ).join('\n');
6     return `
7       <html>
8       <head>
9         <meta http-equiv="Content-Type" content="text/html; charset=UTF-8" />
10      </head>
11      <body>
12      <form action="${form.url}" method="post" enctype="multipart/form-data">
13      ${fields}
14      Select a JPG file:
15      <input type="file" name="file" /> <br />
16      <input type="submit" name="submit" value="Upload file" />
17      </form>
18      </html>
19    `;
20  };
```

To complete the form display function, we'll need to set up the AWS S3 object and configure allowed capacity for uploads. Let's use another CloudFormation parameter for this, so the function just needs to read the value from an environment variable. The full function will look like in the next listing:

──────────────── ch8/user-form/show-form.js ────────────────

```
1   const htmlResponse = require('./html-response');
2   const buildForm = require('./build-form');
3   const aws = require('aws-sdk');
4   const s3 = new aws.S3();
5   const uploadLimitInMB = parseInt(process.env.UPLOAD_LIMIT_IN_MB);
```

────────────────────────

[3]https://docs.aws.amazon.com/AmazonS3/latest/API/sigv4-HTTPPOSTForms.html

```
6  exports.lambdaHandler = async (event, context) => {
7    const apiHost = event.requestContext.domainName,
8      prefix = event.requestContext.stage,
9      redirectUrl = `https://${apiHost}/${prefix}/confirm`,
10     params = {
11       Bucket: process.env.UPLOAD_S3_BUCKET,
12       Expires: 600,
13       Conditions: [
14         ['content-length-range', 1, uploadLimitInMB * 1000000],
15       ],
16       Fields: {
17         success_action_redirect: redirectUrl,
18         acl: 'private',
19         key: context.awsRequestId + '.jpg'
20       }
21     },
22     form = s3.createPresignedPost(params);
23   return htmlResponse(buildForm(form));
24 };
```

Let's add an additional parameter for the maximum upload size to our template. Include the block from the following listing in the Parameters section of the template, indented one level (so that UploadLimitInMb aligns with AppStage, which we added in the previous chapter).

—————————— ch8/template.yaml ——————————

```
13  UploadLimitInMb:
14    Type: Number
15    Default: 5
16    Description: Maximum upload size in megabytes
17    MinValue: 1
18    MaxValue: 100
```

Signed download URLs

In the previous chapter, we used the same URL for both the form display function and the form processing function. This was possible because the browser web form workflow used two different HTTP methods. To display the form, it sent a GET request. To upload the submission details, it sent a POST request. Because S3 redirects work as GET method calls, we cannot use the same URL with different methods any more. The browser will send a POST request directly to S3, which will redirect to another URL. We'll need a different URL to handle that redirect, so let's create a new API endpoint.

When S3 sends a redirect after the upload, it will include information about the uploaded file in the query string. This allows us to do some post-processing on the uploaded file or to let the users access it. To keep things simple for now, let's just allow users to download a file they uploaded. In theory, we could read the file out using a Lambda function and send it back through API Gateway. By now, you know that there is a better way to handle that.

S3 can serve public files directly to browsers. For example, public files in a bucket called testbucket in the us-east-1 region will be accessible directly from https://testbucket.s3.amazonaws.com. For other regions, the second URL component is s3- followed by the region (for example https://testbucket.s3-eu-west-1.amazonaws.com). Letting users download files is a great option if you don't care about protecting read access, for example if you are making a public gallery. To upload publicly readable files, just change the access control list in the upload policy from private to public-read (line 18 in show-form.js).

To tightly control who can read the uploaded files, instead of a public link we can pre-sign a download request. A signed download request effectively provides a temporary grant to access a particular file on S3 directly. Similar to file uploads, directly downloading files from S3 is so common that the AWS SDK has a shortcut operation for it. We can use s3.getSignedUrl to sign generic S3 requests. We need to give it the related object key and expiry time for the grant, and specify the type of the S3 REST API operation. For retrieving objects, the REST API operation is called getObject. The signature method returns a URL with query string parameters prepared according to the authorised grant.

Create a new file in the Lambda code directory, called confirm-upload.js, using the following listing:

────────────────────────────────── ch8/user-form/confirm-upload.js ──────────────────────────────────

```
const htmlResponse = require('./html-response');
const aws = require('aws-sdk');
const s3 = new aws.S3();

exports.lambdaHandler = async (event, context) => {
  const params = {
    Bucket: process.env.UPLOAD_S3_BUCKET,
    Key: event.queryStringParameters.key,
    Expires: 600
  };
  const url = s3.getSignedUrl('getObject', params);
  const responseText = `
    <html><body>
    <h1>Thanks</h1>
    <a href="${url}">
      check your upload
    </a>
        (the link expires in 10 minutes)
    </body></html>
  `;
  return htmlResponse(responseText);
};
```

──

Although the signing methods allow us to specify arbitrary expiry periods, if the credentials used to sign a request expire before the policy, the signature will no longer be valid. Lambda functions work under temporary credentials that are only valid for a short period. AWS does not publish any data about this officially, but my tests suggest that this period is 10 to 20 minutes. This is fine for immediate operations, but not much more. If you need to generate signed URLs that last longer, you'll need to create a separate IAM user, allow it access to the bucket, generate a set of AWS access keys for the user, and then instantiate the S3 service object in Lambda using those credentials.

Protecting S3 files

Users can now upload files, but they may rightly be concerned about security and privacy. Let's encrypt the file contents to protect them. In a typical three-tier server application, an application server could receive the user data and then encrypt it before saving to S3. With a direct upload, we can't control what is sent to S3, because we've removed the gatekeeper. We could try encrypting this on the client device before sending, but then we couldn't use just a simple browser form. Plus we'd have to somehow send our encryption keys to client devices, which can create a security nightmare. Because encryption was such a common need, AWS implemented it as part of the platform. With serverless architectures, most gatekeeper roles pass on to the platform, not to a Lambda function.

You can just flip a switch and all newly created files on S3 will be encrypted at rest, regardless of where they come from. With CloudFormation, that switch is behind the BucketEncryption property of the AWS::S3::Bucket resource. Change the template resource definition for the bucket to be like that in the next listing:

—————————————————————— ch8/template.yaml ——————————————————————

```
 9   Resources:
10     UploadS3Bucket:
11       Type: AWS::S3::Bucket
 2       Properties:
13         BucketEncryption:
14           ServerSideEncryptionConfiguration:
15             - ServerSideEncryptionByDefault:
16                 SSEAlgorithm: AES256
```

Once activated, server-side encryption works without any changes to client code. As objects are uploaded, S3 will encrypt them before storage, and decrypt before sending back to client code. In this case, we're letting S3 create an encryption key for our account and use it without any special configuration. When S3 manages the encryption keys, there is no special cost for automatically encrypting or decrypting content. You can, of course, set your own encryption keys if you need a higher level of security. For more information, check out the section *Protecting Data Using Server-Side Encryption*[4] in the AWS S3 documentation.

To finish things off and deploy this version of the functions, we'll need to rewrite the template significantly. We can leave the web API as it was in the previous chapter, but we'll have to reconfigure the functions. The function that displays the web form now needs full access to the bucket, because it will need to generate

————————————————————

[4]https://docs.aws.amazon.com/AmazonS3/latest/dev/serv-side-encryption.html

upload signatures. We also need to pass the bucket name and allowed upload size as environment variables. Modify the function template to look like the next listing:

──────────────── ch8/template.yaml ────────────────

```
31  ShowFormFunction:
32    Type: AWS::Serverless::Function
33    Properties:
34      CodeUri: user-form/
35      Handler: show-form.lambdaHandler
36      Runtime: nodejs12.x
37      Events:
38        ShowForm:
39          Type: Api
40          Properties:
41            Path: /
42            Method: get
43            RestApiId: !Ref WebApi
44      Environment:
45        Variables:
46          UPLOAD_S3_BUCKET: !Ref UploadS3Bucket
47          UPLOAD_LIMIT_IN_MB: !Ref UploadLimitInMb
48      Policies:
49        - S3FullAccessPolicy:
50            BucketName: !Ref UploadS3Bucket
```

The function that showed a thank-you note now does a lot more, so let's rename it to reflect the new responsibilities. We changed the JavaScript file name for the function, so we'll need to upload the Handler property accordingly. Also, we need this function to respond to the /confirm URL, so update the Path property in the event.

Finally, because it only needs to sign a download URL, there's no need to keep full bucket access for this function. We can reduce it to read-only access and tighten up security. SAM has a convenient template policy for this as well, called S3ReadPolicy. Change the function template according to the next listing:

──────────────── ch8/template.yaml ────────────────

```
51  ConfirmUploadFunction:
52    Type: AWS::Serverless::Function
53    Properties:
54      CodeUri: user-form/
55      Handler: confirm-upload.lambdaHandler
56      Runtime: nodejs12.x
57      Events:
58        ConfirmForm:
59          Type: Api
60          Properties:
61            Path: /confirm
```

```
        Method: get
        RestApiId: !Ref WebApi
    Environment:
      Variables:
        UPLOAD_S3_BUCKET: !Ref UploadS3Bucket
    Policies:
      - S3ReadPolicy:
          BucketName: !Ref UploadS3Bucket
```

We've not added any important new resources in this chapter, so the Outputs section of the file can remain as before. Build, package and deploy the stack, and then open the API URL in a browser. You should see a form with a button to select a file (Figure 8.2).

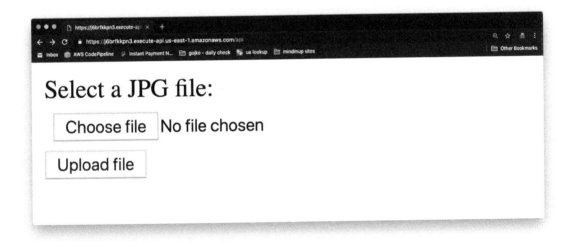

Figure 8.2: *The display form function shows an HTML form with the upload policy in hidden fields, ready to process a file upload.*

Select an image file from your local disk using the *Choose File* button then click the *Upload file* button to send it to S3. If you monitor the network requests in your browser, you'll see a connection directly to S3 to transfer the file.

Once the upload completes, your browser will redirect to the confirmation page. The download link on that page allows you to immediately check that the upload was processed correctly.

Of course, just letting people upload files and download them back isn't particularly useful. In Chapter 9, we'll set up a service process to handle uploads. In Chapter 10, we'll extend the process to produce thumbnails from uploaded images.

Interesting experiments

- Try uploading a file larger than 5 megabytes (maximum specified in `UploadLimitInMb`).
- Change the `show-form.js` script to shorten the signature expiry period. Redeploy the application and open the initial upload page, then wait until the link expires and try uploading a file.

9. Handling platform events

This chapter explains how to trigger Lambda functions after platform events such as file uploads to S3. You will also learn about the difference between synchronous and asynchronous Lambda invocations.

The stack we deployed in the previous chapter lets users upload files quickly and easily, but the application does not do anything with those files. We have several options for how to process the uploads.

The first option would be to create an API endpoint backed by a Lambda function that synchronously converts image files into thumbnails. It could send the outputs back to users directly or save the output to S3 and redirect users to the result location. The advantage of this option is that it would be very simple. The major disadvantage is that it would not work for large files. API Gateway will stop requests that take longer than 29 seconds. Lambda functions can work for much longer, up to 15 minutes, but API Gateway does not allow long-running tasks. If you find yourself hitting this limit, instead of trying to work around it, think about solving it with a different design. Long-running HTTP requests are liable to get interrupted. The longer the request, the more likely that unreliable coffee-shop WiFi networks might restart, user devices might try to conserve battery and suspend network actions, or phones switch from mobile networks to home WiFi and change IP addresses. Don't make people wait over HTTP.

The second option would be to handle the conversion asynchronously. In a typical three-tier server app, the usual way of handling long-running tasks would be to create several API endpoints. The first endpoint would start a background task and send the task reference back to the client. The second endpoint would allow the client to check the status of a job using the reference. The client could then deal with intermittent network problems without losing access to the results. A third endpoint would allow the client to retrieve the outcome using the job reference once the task is finished. We could do something very similar with several API Gateway resources and Lambda functions, but this would be much more expensive than it needs to be. We can make the application cheaper and faster by incorporating serverless design.

In the previous chapter, we removed the need for an application server to work as a gatekeeper, and gave that role to the AWS platform instead. In a similar way, we can move some orchestration tasks from a typical middle-tier application server to the platform itself. This can significantly reduce costs. For example, instead of an API endpoint that allows clients to check whether a conversion task is complete, we could just give the client a pre-signed URL to check for results on S3. With an API endpoint, we'd have to pay for an API call, a Lambda execution, and access to S3 to check for results. With the client going to S3 directly, we only pay for S3 access. The overall usage is much cheaper and there are fewer components in between, reducing end-user latency. Moving to a serverless design makes this operation both cheaper and faster.

Similarly, we do not need a separate endpoint just to start the conversion. Many AWS platform resources can notify Lambda functions about important events. For example, S3 can directly call a Lambda function once a file is uploaded or deleted. There's no need for pay for an additional API call and a Lambda execution just for the client device to notify us that an upload is complete.

The next step for our application is to create a skeleton for asynchronous processing (Figure 9.1). We will introduce another function to act on file uploads, without the limitation of API Gateway call duration. That function will for now just copy the file over to another bucket, so we can test the whole flow. In the previous chapter, we used the upload confirmation function (step 3 in Figure 9.1) to generate a pre-signed URL for files in the upload bucket. We can change the URL to access the files in the results bucket instead. Clients can use that URL to retrieve the results. In Chapter 10 we will make the conversion function actually produce thumbnails.

First, let's create a new function to handle the file conversions. There's no need to mix the source code for the form processing functions with this function, so let's create a new function sub-directory. Make sure your current working directory is the one containing `template.yaml` (if you followed the example in Chapter 2 to create the project, this will be app), and run the following two commands:

```
mkdir image-conversion
cd image-conversion
```

We'll use JavaScript and Node.js for this function. SAM relies on NPM package information to build functions, so let's initialise this directory using NPM:

```
npm init --yes
```

We could have used a different runtime here, because it's a different function and SAM lets you mix functions created with different languages. If JavaScript is not your preferred language, you can also find versions of the same project written in different languages at https://runningserverless.com.

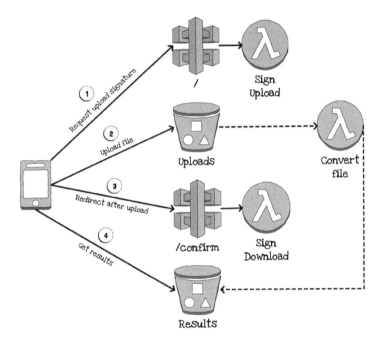

Figure 9.1: *Instead of an application server coordinating actions, S3 will trigger file conversion directly after upload.*

Generating test events

Events coming from S3 will have a different structure to those coming from API Gateway. When we started experimenting with API events in Chapter 6, we used a nice trick to understand the structure: create an empty function that just logs the event to CloudWatch at the start. We could do something similar now, but SAM has another tool that makes this even simpler. We can use `sam local generate-event` to create sample events. For example, run this command to see what an S3 object upload event looks like:

```
sam local generate-event s3 put
```

You can use this trick to generate test events for many AWS services. The first parameter after generate-event is the service name (in this case, s3). The second is the type of the event (in this case, we're looking for put events). To see a full list of services that SAM can generate events for, run the following command:

```
sam local generate-event --help
```

To see a list of events SAM can generate for a particular service, list the service name before --help. For example, to see a list of possible events for s3, run the following command:

```
sam local generate-event s3 --help
```

From the sample event, you can see that the event contains an array of records, with a single element. The record has an s3 property that contains the bucket and object sub-properties. We'll need to pull out the bucket name and the key from the file upload event. Let's create a utility function to extract just the information we need from the event. Add a file called extract-s3-info.js to the new function code directory (image-conversion).

──────────── ch9/image-conversion/extract-s3-info.js ────────────

```
1  module.exports = function extractS3Info(event) {
2    const eventRecord = event.Records && event.Records[0],
3      bucket = eventRecord.s3.bucket.name,
4      key = eventRecord.s3.object.key;
5    return {bucket, key};
6  };
```

Working with files

In Chapter 7, we used a method of the AWS S3 SDK to upload the contents of a string into an S3 bucket. Although we could potentially work with images as in-memory strings or buffers, this would unnecessarily increase the memory footprint of the Lambda function, costing more than it should. The S3 SDK for most languages supports working with file streams.

Our conversion function needs to download an S3 object into a local file, so we can later produce thumbnails. It will also need to upload the resulting file contents to S3. Let's create two utility methods for that. Save the following code as s3-util.js in the conversion function code directory.

──────────── ch9/image-conversion/s3-util.js ────────────

```
1  const aws = require('aws-sdk'),
2    fs = require('fs'),
3    s3 = new aws.S3(),
4    downloadFileFromS3 = function (bucket, fileKey, filePath) {
```

```
      console.log('downloading', bucket, fileKey, filePath);
      return new Promise((resolve, reject) => {
        const file = fs.createWriteStream(filePath),
          stream = s3.getObject({
            Bucket: bucket,
            Key: fileKey
          }).createReadStream();
        stream.on('error', reject);
        file.on('error', reject);
        file.on('finish', () => {
          console.log('downloaded', bucket, fileKey);
          resolve(filePath);
        });
        stream.pipe(file);
      });
    },
  uploadFileToS3 = function (bucket, fileKey, filePath, contentType) {
      console.log('uploading', bucket, fileKey, filePath);
      return s3.upload({
        Bucket: bucket,
        Key: fileKey,
        Body: fs.createReadStream(filePath),
        ACL: 'private',
        ContentType: contentType
      }).promise();
    };

module.exports = {
  downloadFileFromS3: downloadFileFromS3,
  uploadFileToS3: uploadFileToS3
};
```

Whenever we create files in the Lambda container, we also need to consider cleaning up. Although Lambda function calls are independent, they are not stateless. Lambda can choose to reuse a container for the same function configuration. If we get a huge amount of constant traffic, Lambda will reuse the same container over a longer period of time. Our function will download S3 objects into the local file system, so if we never clean up, the local disk might run out of space. Let's add a utility function to delete temporary files. Any problems cleaning up shouldn't really abort processing, so this function can safely ignore errors. Save the code from the next listing into silent-remove.js in the conversion function code directory.

──────────────── ch9/image-conversion/silent-remove.js ────────────────

```
1  const util = require('util'),
2    fs = require('fs'),
3    removeAsync = util.promisify(fs.unlink);
4  module.exports = async function silentRemove(file) {
```

```
5    try {
6      await removeAsync(file);
7    } catch (e) {
8      // ignore error
9    }
10   };
```

Working with asynchronous events

The Lambda interface is always the same, regardless of the event source or type. The conversion function will expect the same two parameters as all our Lambda functions so far: the event and the context object. But unlike everything else we've done so far in the book, the Lambda function won't be able to just return the result back to the client. That's because S3 invokes the Lambda function in the background, separately from the client request going through API Gateway.

AWS Lambda functions support two types of call, synchronous and asynchronous:

- Synchronous calls expect the caller to wait until the Lambda function completes. The function reports the result directly to the caller. API Gateway uses this method.
- Asynchronous calls complete immediately, and the Lambda function keeps running in the background. The function can't send the result directly to the caller (it's 'fire and forget'). S3 and most other platform services use this method.

With asynchronous calls, the function also needs to be responsible for storing the output somewhere. The usual way to achieve this is to somehow correlate outputs with inputs, for example including the target output location in the event parameters, or deriving the result location from inputs. In this case, an easy solution for that would be to use a different bucket for results, and store the output using the same key as the input. Buckets are effectively namespaces for files, and two different files can have the same keys in different buckets. We'll just need to tell the function about the result bucket name. For that, we can use an environment variable. Create a new file for the main Lambda function, for example index.js, in the conversion function source directory.

—————————————————————— ch9/image-conversion/index.js ——————————————————————

```
1    const path = require('path'),
2      os = require('os'),
3      s3Util = require('./s3-util'),
4      extractS3Info = require('./extract-s3-info'),
5      silentRemove = require('./silent-remove'),
6      OUTPUT_BUCKET = process.env.OUTPUT_BUCKET,
7      supportedFormats = ['jpg', 'jpeg', 'png', 'gif'];
```

```
18
19   exports.handler = async (event, context) => {
20     const s3Info = extractS3Info(event),
21       id = context.awsRequestId,
22       extension = path.extname(s3Info.key).toLowerCase(),
23       tempFile = path.join(os.tmpdir(), id + extension),
24       extensionWithoutDot = extension.slice(1),
25       contentType = `image/${extensionWithoutDot}`;
16     console.log('converting', s3Info.bucket, ':', s3Info.key, 'using', tempFile);
17     if (!supportedFormats.includes(extensionWithoutDot)) {
18       throw new Error(`unsupported file type ${extension}`);
19     }
20     await s3Util.downloadFileFromS3(s3Info.bucket, s3Info.key, tempFile);
21     // in the next chapter, we'll do something useful with the tempfile here...
22     await s3Util.uploadFileToS3(OUTPUT_BUCKET, s3Info.key, tempFile, contentType);
23     await silentRemove(tempFile);
24   };
```

This function requires another bucket to store results, so let's add it to the template. Add the following lines to the Resources section of your template (at the same indentation level as UploadS3Bucket).

──────────────── ch9/template.yaml ────────────────

```
27   ThumbnailsS3Bucket:
28     Type: AWS::S3::Bucket
29     Properties:
30       BucketEncryption:
31         ServerSideEncryptionConfiguration:
32           - ServerSideEncryptionByDefault:
33               SSEAlgorithm: AES256
```

The web API and the form display function don't need to change, but the confirm upload function should now generate download signatures for the results bucket. We can keep the same source code, but we'll need to reconfigure it with the results bucket. Change the ConfirmUploadFunction configuration to update the bucket references (lines 73 and 76 in the next code listing).

──────────────── ch9/template.yaml ────────────────

```
58   ConfirmUploadFunction:
59     Type: AWS::Serverless::Function
60     Properties:
61       CodeUri: user-form/
62       Handler: confirm-upload.lambdaHandler
63       Runtime: nodejs12.x
64       Events:
65         ConfirmForm:
66           Type: Api
```

```
67            Properties:
68              Path: /confirm
69              Method: get
70              RestApiId: !Ref WebApi
71        Environment:
72          Variables:
73            UPLOAD_S3_BUCKET: !Ref ThumbnailsS3Bucket
74        Policies:
75          - S3ReadPolicy:
76              BucketName: !Ref ThumbnailsS3Bucket
```

Next, we need to add a new function for the file conversion. Create a new AWS::Serverless::Function resource according to the following listing in the Resources section of your template (at the same indentation level as ConfirmUploadFunction).

────────────────────── ch9/template.yaml ──────────────────────

```
77  ConvertFileFunction:
78    Type: AWS::Serverless::Function
79    Properties:
80      CodeUri: image-conversion/
81      Handler: index.handler
82      Runtime: nodejs12.x
83      Events:
84        FileUploaded:
85          Type: S3
86          Properties:
87            Bucket: !Ref UploadS3Bucket
88            Events: s3:ObjectCreated:*
89      Timeout: 600
90      Environment:
91        Variables:
92          OUTPUT_BUCKET: !Ref ThumbnailsS3Bucket
93      Policies:
94        - S3FullAccessPolicy:
95            BucketName: !Ref ThumbnailsS3Bucket
```

Here are some important settings:

- CodeUri (line 80) points to the directory with the function source code. In the previous sections we used image-conversion.
- Handler (line 81) specifies the module and the function name. Earlier in this section, I suggested saving the main Lambda code in the index module (index.js file), in a function called handler, so the full Handler value should be index.handler.
- This function needs to work on relatively large files, so remember to set the Timeout property (line 89), for example to 600 seconds.

- The source code expects the results bucket name in the OUTPUT_BUCKET environment variable, so we need to configure that as well in the template (lines 90-92). We can use !Ref to turn the internal bucket reference into the actual bucket name.
- We also need to let the function write to the results bucket (lines 93-95).

Avoiding circular references

The conversion function also needs permissions to read from the uploads bucket, but allowing that won't be as easy as before. You can try adding another read policy into this list, but CFN Lint will complain about a circular reference. Try deploying it to CloudFormation, and you'll get the same error.

This is because SAM sets up Lambda function policies together with the IAM role for the function. To set up the function, it needs to set up the role first. To set up the role, it would need to know about the target buckets for the permissions. On the other hand, SAM sets up bucket lifecycle events, such as invoking Lambda functions, together with the bucket. So in order to set up the upload bucket, it would need to know the function reference expecting bucket events. So the upload bucket depends on the conversion function, which depends on the role, which depends on the bucket. Hence the circular dependency.

We could in theory break this circle by letting the Lambda read from all the buckets, but that's a horrible thing to do from a security perspective. Instead, we'll set a custom IAM policy and not use SAM templates. This is why I left out the uploads bucket permission from the previous listing, specifying the conversion function. SAM can then create the function role, then the conversion function, then the bucket lifecycle events, and then append a policy to an existing role. That way, the function and the role will not depend on buckets during creation.

Setting custom IAM policies

CloudFormation has a resource for attaching policies to existing roles, AWS::IAM::Policy. We can specify an IAM policy that lets the role execute s3:GetObject on any resource in the target bucket, and attach it to the role after both the bucket and the role are created. The policy would depend both on the role and the bucket, but nothing would depend on the policy itself. Add the following lines to the Resources section of the template (at the same indentation level as ConvertFileFunction).

─────────────── ch9/template.yaml ───────────────

```
96  ConvertFunctionCanReadUploads:
97    Type: AWS::IAM::Policy
98    Properties:
99      PolicyName: ConvertFunctionCanReadUploads
00      PolicyDocument:
01        Version: '2012-10-17'
02        Statement:
03          - Effect: Allow
```

```
104          Action:
105            - "s3:GetObject"
106          Resource:
107            - !Sub "${UploadS3Bucket.Arn}/*"
108      Roles:
109        - !Ref ConvertFileFunctionRole
```

With S3 policies that apply to objects, we can specify a pattern for objects, in the form of `Bucket ARN/Key`. As usual for IAM policies, we can use an asterisk (*) to match any value. CloudFormation S3 bucket resources have a `.Arn` property that contains the ARN of the bucket. So `!Sub "${UploadS3Bucket.Arn}/*"` (line 107) effectively means any object in the upload bucket.

Notice the reference `ConvertFileFunctionRole` on line 109. We do not have an object called that anywhere in the template, so this might seem like an error. Unless you tell SAM to use a specific role for a function, it will create a new IAM role implicitly. SAM puts the role ID into a new CloudFormation reference named after the function but with the `Role` suffix. So the implicitly created role for `ConvertFileFunction` ends up being called `ConvertFileFunctionRole`.

Build, package and deploy the stack now. Set up a log tail for the conversion function, so you can see it in action:

```
sam logs -n ConvertFileFunction --stack-name sam-test-1 --tail
```

You should be able to upload a JPG, PNG or GIF image, watch the logs to know when the file is copied to S3, then click the link shown by the confirmation function. That link will display a copy of the original image, from the results bucket. In the next chapter, we'll make the application resize the images in this step.

Of course, watching logs is not a nice user experience. We could easily adjust the client code to poll for the result using the signed URL and display a nice message while the background task is still running. There is, however, a big problem with that approach. Try uploading a file that's not an image. You'll see it explode in the logs, but the client has no idea about it. That's because S3 is using asynchronous events.

Handling asynchronous errors with dead letters

With synchronous calls, errors can be reported directly back to the caller, and the caller can then decide whether it's worth retrying or not. With asynchronous calls, the caller can't do that, because it is not waiting on results.

The good news is that to protect you against intermittent network problems or transient infrastructure issues, Lambda will automatically retry twice. AWS does not publish any official documentation on the duration between retries, but my experience is that the first retry will happen almost immediately after an error. If the function fails to process the event again, the second retry will happen about a minute later. Keep watching the logs while Lambda refuses to copy a file that's not an image, and you'll see the retries.

Asynchronous request IDs and retries

If Lambda retries processing an event, it will send the same request ID as in the original attempt. You can use the request ID to check for any partial results if your Lambda works in multiple stages, and then just partially re-process the event. This is another reason why it's good to use request IDs to generate resource references.

If the second retry fails as well, Lambda gives up on processing the event, concluding that the error is in the code rather than the infrastructure, or that the infrastructure has not recovered quickly enough. If events don't work after two retries, it often means that we made some bad assumptions about the potential contents, for example that people will always upload images. I like to know about such events, especially while I am still developing something, so I can handle those cases better.

You can configure the allowed number of retries and the maximum waiting time for a request to be processed using the `MaximumRetryAttempts` and `MaximumRetryAttempts` parameters of a function. If you use the low-level CloudFormation resource (`AWS::Lambda::Function`), apply these properties directly to the function. For the SAM wrapper (`AWS::Serverless::Function`), these properties are sub-parameters of `EventInvokeConfig`. For more information configuring retry policies with SAM and an example, check out the `EventInvokeConfiguration` documentation page[1] in the SAM Developer guide.

In Chapter 5, I mentioned that CloudWatch automatically tracks errors for Lambda functions. Although we can see statistics about failed retry errors in the CloudWatch console, we won't be able to see the actual contents of the events that caused problems there. However, failed events aren't necessarily lost forever; you can configure Lambda to send them to a *dead letter queue*. You can then set up additional processing or a custom retrial. For example, send the caller an error report, notify support staff about the problem, or even delay the event for a few minutes and then send it back to the same function.

Lambda can use two types of dead letter queues: Amazon Simple Queue Service (SQS) or Amazon Simple Notification Service (SNS). The two types of queues are importantly different in how they deal with message delivery. SNS is a better choice for instant processing. SQS is a better choice for offline or batch processing.

SQS will store the message for a listener to retrieve it. If nobody is listening when a message arrives, SQS will keep it in the queue. SQS consumers compete for messages, so if there are many listeners, only one will get the chance to process a single message.

SNS will just ignore a message if it has no subscriptions when the message arrives. It will send each message to all active subscriptions. If there are many listeners, everyone gets a copy.

Let's set up a dead letter queue that sends us an email if there are problems. For that, we don't really need batch processing, so SNS is a better choice.

If neither SNS or SQS fit your usage needs for dead letter queues, you can configure an alternative *Lambda destination* for errors. Lambda Destinations were introduced in November 2019, and allow users to forward

---

[1]https://docs.aws.amazon.com/serverless-application-model/latest/developerguide/sam-property-function-eventinvokeconfiguration.html

results or error messages from a Lambda function somewhere else. Configuring a destination for errors is similar to setting up a dead letter queue, but supports more AWS services, including directly invoking another Lambda function or sending an event to AWS EventBridge. For more information on AWS destinations, check out the *Configuring Destinations* section of the *Asynchronous Invocation* page[2] in the AWS Lambda Developer Guide.

Building from a different template

If you are using the source code package from https://runningserverless.com, the main template file is without the dead letter queue in the directory for this chapter. The one with the dead letter queue configuration is `template-with-dlq.yaml`. Remember to use `-t` to tell SAM to build it from a particular file, so use `sam build -t template-with-dlq.yaml`.

Add a resource of type `AWS::SNS::Topic` to the template resources section (at the same indentation level as `ConvertFileFunction`).

———————————————————— ch9/template-with-dlq.yaml ————————————————————

```
126  NotifyAdmins:
127    Type: AWS::SNS::Topic
```

To send dead letters from the `ConvertFileFunction` to the SNS topic, add the following three lines to the function template properties (at the same indentation level as `Policies`, for example).

———————————————————— ch9/template-with-dlq.yaml ————————————————————

```
123  DeadLetterQueue:
124    Type: SNS
125    TargetArn: !Ref NotifyAdmins
```

The nice thing about SAM and dead letter queues is that SAM will automatically set the permissions for a Lambda function to publish messages to the target queue. If you're using CloudFormation Lambda functions directly without SAM, you'll need to add the permissions yourself.

SNS can send messages to Lambda functions, so we could now implement another function that acts on notification about potential problems. SNS can also send messages by email, which is great for troubleshooting failed events during development. We now have a dead letter queue set up, so anyone can manually subscribe to the topic from the SNS Web Console[3] and receive email notifications about any unexpected problems.

With many developers working in a team and people trying lots of different things out, the notifications can get quite frequent. It would be much better if people got notifications only for their own experiments. We can do that by setting up the SNS subscription directly in the template, based on a deployment parameter.

---

[2]https://docs.aws.amazon.com/lambda/latest/dg/invocation-async.html
[3]https://console.aws.amazon.com/sns/

Each developer can then set up the subscription automatically with their own email when deploying the stack.

Let's add another parameter for the email. Add the following lines to the Parameters section of the template.

——————————————— ch9/template-with-dlq.yaml ———————————————

```
ContactEmailAddress:
  Type: String
  Description: Email address for operational notifications
  Default: ''
```

Conditional resources

Email subscriptions are not the right solution for production deployments. Emailing each individual event would most likely cause too much noise, and people will just start ignoring that. It would be much better to set up error logging completely differently. So let's make the email subscription optional by adding a condition to our resource.

CloudFormation can activate or deactivate resources based on certain conditions, which we need to set up in a separate template section titled Conditions. I usually put this between parameters and resources. Add the following lines to your template as a top-level section, for example above Resources.

——————————————— ch9/template-with-dlq.yaml ———————————————

```
Conditions:
  ContactEmailSet: !Not [ !Equals ['', !Ref ContactEmailAddress]]
```

The previous listing creates a condition to check whether the parameter ContactEmailAddress has a value, or more precisely to check that it does not equal a blank string. For functions with multiple parameters, or to specify the order of execution, CloudFormation uses square brackets ([]). !Not and !Equals are built-in functions with fairly obvious purposes. For more information on other functions you can use, check out the AWS CloudFormation *Condition Functions*[4] reference page.

We can use conditions to include or exclude resources from a deployed application by adding a Condition field below the resource header (at same indentation level as Type). For example, add the following code to the resources section of your template to create a conditional email subscription (at the same indentation level as the SNS topic, for example).

——————————————— ch9/template-with-dlq.yaml ———————————————

```
AlarmNotifyOpsSubscription:
  Type: AWS::SNS::Subscription
  Condition: ContactEmailSet
  Properties:
```

---

[4]https://docs.aws.amazon.com/AWSCloudFormation/latest/UserGuide/intrinsic-function-reference-conditions.html

```
144        Endpoint: !Ref ContactEmailAddress
145        Protocol: email
146        TopicArn: !Ref NotifyAdmins
```

Build, package and deploy the stack without setting the email, and CloudFormation will not set up the subscription at all. You can confirm that by listing the stack resources from the command line, or by inspecting the stack from the AWS CloudFormation Web Console.

Then deploy again, but provide an email (no need to package and build the stack again; we're using the same template). You can set the email using --parameter-overrides:

```
sam deploy --template-file output.yaml --stack-name sam-test-1 --capabilities CAPABILITY_IAM
↳    --parameter-overrides ContactEmailAddress=YOUR_EMAIL
```

Check the stack resources after the deployment, and you'll see the subscription object there. Email subscriptions are not automatically active, to prevent spam, but if you check your email, you'll see a notification from AWS asking you to confirm the subscription (Figure 9.2).

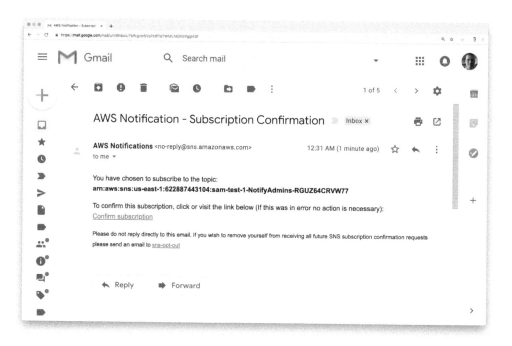

Figure 9.2: *SNS sends a request to confirm a new email subscription to the dead letter queue.*

Click the confirmation link in the email to set up the subscription. After that, try uploading a file that is not an image to the conversion application. You will see two retries in the logs, and, after that, SNS will send you the failed event (Figure 9.3).

This is a great way to catch unexpected issues during testing, so we can then learn about them and handle such errors better in the code. Dead letter queues will also catch timeouts, so you'll know that some function needs to be reconfigured so it can run longer, or alternatively be optimised to run faster.

We can use this same dead letter queue for as many functions as we like now. There's not much point setting this up for events triggered by API Gateway, because it uses synchronous invocations, so Lambda sends errors directly to the caller instead. At the time when I wrote this, dead letters and Lambda destinations worked only for asynchronous calls.

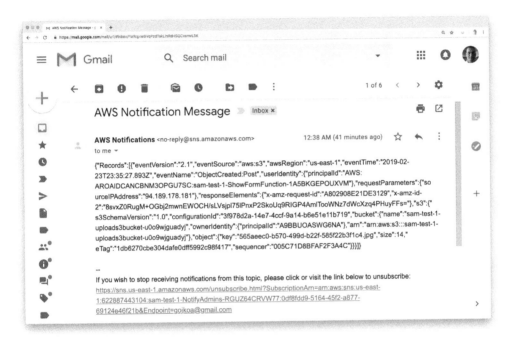

Figure 9.3: *Failed events are no longer lost, but sent by email to developers.*

Interesting experiments

- Try adding a development dependency to a Lambda function, for example a unit testing library, and check whether it is packaged with your function by sam build.
- Try configuring a non-existent dependency directly in package.json for one of your functions, and check how sam build handles the error.
- Try creating a different function that will automatically be executed from the dead letter queue SNS notification.
- Try configuring the supported file types in the application template and passing the file types to the conversion function as a parameter.

Part III

Designing serverless applications

10. Using application components

This chapter explains how to compose applications from third-party components by using Lambda layers. You will also learn about the AWS Serverless Application Repository, a public library of reusable application templates.

In the previous chapter, we built a skeleton for asynchronous processing. In this chapter, we'll use that structure to create thumbnails from uploaded images. JavaScript isn't really designed for working with binary files, and it would be better if we used a low-level system utility for image processing. For example, the mogrify[1] command line utility from the ImageMagick package can transform a wide range of image formats and is very easy to use. To modify a file into a thumbnail version, we can just use the -thumbnail option. Mogrify understands resolutions in the format Width x Height, but it can preserve aspect ratios if we provide only the width followed by the letter x. For example, to convert an image file into a 300 pixel wide thumbnail, we just need to run the following command:

```
mogrify -thumbnail 300x <FILE>
```

Different people might want to set up different thumbnail sizes, so let's add parameter for that into our template. Add the block from the following listing to the Parameters section of your template, at the same indentation level as other parameter definitions (for example, UploadLimitInMb).

─────────────────────────── ch10/template.yaml ───────────────────────────

```
19  ThumbnailWidth:
20    Type: Number
21    Default: 300
22    Description: Thumbnail width in pixels
23    MinValue: 10
24    MaxValue: 1000
```

Lambda runs a reduced version of Amazon Linux, a clone of CentOS, which is itself a clone of Red Hat Enterprise Linux. ImageMagick tools are usually present on Linux systems; however, they are not included in the more recent Lambda environments. Up until the Node.js 8 Lambda runtime, Lambda containers also included ImageMagick tools. In order to improve start-up performance, the standard Lambda environment comes with only the essential system libraries. In order to use mogrify, we'll have to add that binary tool to the Lambda virtual machines running our conversion function.

The AWS Serverless Application Repository

The *AWS Serverless Application Repository*[2] (SAR) is a library of AWS SAM applications (or, more correctly, it is a library of SAM application components). SAR has two primary purposes. The first is to enable organisations to share reusable components internally, so teams can easily deploy infrastructural templates built by other teams. The second is to work as a public library, making a few hundred open-source components available to everyone.

---

[1]https://imagemagick.org/script/mogrify.php
[2]https://serverlessrepo.aws.amazon.com/applications

The public part of the SAR makes it easy to discover blueprints for applications, to find integration components for third-party services and to set up utility resources (Figure 10.1). Some of these applications were published by AWS, and some by third-party developers. In order to handle image conversions with the new Lambda runtimes in MindMup, I had to package ImageMagick as a SAM component[3]. I then published it to SAR so anyone can get started with image conversions in Lambda easily. You will find that component by searching for image-magick-lambda-layer in the repository.

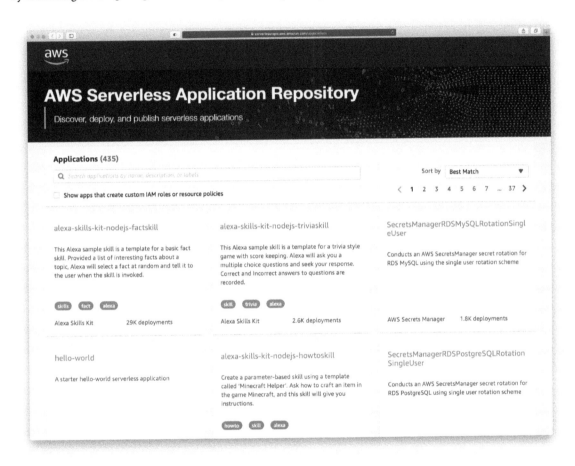

Figure 10.1: *The SAR makes it easy to discover third-party components for SAM applications.*

The SAR makes it easy to deploy pre-packaged components into your AWS account. Find something interesting using the repository web page then click the *Deploy* button. Perhaps more interestingly, it's also possible to directly include anything published to SAR in a SAM application. Technically, a SAR component is just a published CloudFormation template, and it can be embedded in other templates. The marketing term AWS uses for such reused components is *nested applications*. To import a SAR component into a SAM template, we just need to declare a resource with the type AWS::Serverless::Application and point to the application ID and required application version.

---

[3]https://github.com/serverlesspub/imagemagick-aws-lambda-2

For example, to deploy version 1.0.0 of the `image-magick-lambda-layer` SAR component, just add the following lines to your application template, in the Resources section (at the same indentation level as other resources, for example `WebApi`).

———————————————————— ch10/template.yaml ————————————————————

```
83  ImageMagick:
84    Type: AWS::Serverless::Application
85    Properties:
86      Location:
87        ApplicationId:
    ↳   arn:aws:serverlessrepo:us-east-1:145266761615:applications/image-magick-lambda-layer
88        SemanticVersion: 1.0.0
```

Compiling binary tools

One of the best aspects of Linux software is that most of it is open source. If you want to use a binary tool that is not available from the SAR, you can compile it for the correct operating system version and deploy as part of your Lambda function. A great starting point for that is to use the Docker container images from the LambCI project, available from https://github.com/lambci/docker-lambda. They are intended to simulate Lambda runtimes in continuous integration environments, but can also be used to ensure that you are building a binary tool using the correct system libraries for a Lambda runtime environment.

Michael Hart, the author of the LambCI project, even provided a set of templates for compiling many standard Linux tools using the RPM package format. For more information, see the Yumda project https://github.com/lambci/yumda on GitHub.

Lambda layers

The `image-magick-lambda-layer` SAR component makes ImageMagick utilities available to Lambda functions in the form of a layer. A *Lambda layer* is a file package that can be deployed to AWS and then attached to many functions. Layers are useful for sharing large packages across functions and for speeding up deployments. For example, ImageMagick tools consume about 60 MB of file storage. Instead of including them with every single Lambda function that needs access to ImageMagick, we could pack and deploy those tools once in a layer. Individual function packages can then contain only the source code unique to each use case and can request access to image conversion tools during deployment.

From the perspective of a Lambda function, a layer is effectively a shared read-only file system. Files from a layer appear in the /opt directory of the Lambda virtual machine, and we can access them as if they were included in the function itself. For example, once we link the ImageMagick layer, the `mogrify` utility will be in /opt/bin/mogrify.

A single function can attach only up to five layers. Although layers deploy separately from functions, the attached layer size counts towards the total Lambda size. The total unpacked size of the function, including all linked layers, has to be less than 250 MB. Layers do, however, significantly reduce overall consumed deployment capacity for an AWS account. For more information on layers and general Lambda size restrictions, check out the *AWS Lambda Limits*[4] page in the AWS documentation.

Linking functions with layers

Layers, similarly to functions, get a numerically incremental version every time they are published. Unlike Lambda functions, there are no textual aliases for numerical layer versions, so it's not possible to mark a current or latest version easily or to use labels to differentiate between production and testing layer versions. This is a serious limitation, and it's logical to expect AWS to provide a better solution in the future, but at the time when I wrote this, a function had to specify the exact version of a layer it wanted to use. That's why you'll see lots of references to LayerVersion resources.

To attach a version of a layer to a function, use the Layers property of the AWS::Serverless::Function resource. The property needs to be formatted as a list of ARN identifiers of layer versions, even if you want to attach just a single layer. To get the ARN of the layer version created by the ImageMagick nested application, use the ImageMagick.Outputs.LayerVersion reference. Let's decompose that for easier understanding:

1. The first part, ImageMagick, is the name of the resource in our template we used to import the SAR component. It is just a local name we use in our template, and does not need to match the remote application name.
2. The middle part, Outputs, is how we can tell CloudFormation to look into the outputs of an embedded template. You will always use this to read outputs from nested applications.
3. The final part, LayerVersion, is how the nested template called the output containing the layer version. This is specific to a particular application, and you will likely use a different name when importing a different component.

Check out the source code[5] for the embedded template on GitHub, and you'll see a section declaring that output.

> ## SAR application outputs
>
> Remember that we used template outputs in our application to make it easier for client code to learn about important resources such as the web page URL. Nested applications are just CloudFormation templates, and they can provide outputs for that same purpose.

Let's attach the layer to our ConvertFileFunction resource and also pass the new parameter for thumbnail width that we added earlier in this chapter. Because we'll now actually convert files, it is also good to give this function a bit more memory. This will speed up execution significantly. Modify the function template to look similar to the following listing (the important additions are lines 102, 106, 110 and 111).

---

[4]https://docs.aws.amazon.com/lambda/latest/dg/limits.html
[5]https://github.com/serverlesspub/imagemagick-aws-lambda-2/blob/master/template.yaml

--------------------------------- ch10/template.yaml ---------------------------------

```
 89  ConvertFileFunction:
 90    Type: AWS::Serverless::Function
 91    Properties:
 92      CodeUri: image-conversion/
 93      Handler: index.handler
 94      Runtime: nodejs12.x
 95      Events:
 96        FileUploaded:
 97          Type: S3
 98          Properties:
 99            Bucket: !Ref UploadS3Bucket
100            Events: s3:ObjectCreated:*
101      Timeout: 600
102      MemorySize: 1024
103      Environment:
104        Variables:
105          OUTPUT_BUCKET: !Ref ThumbnailsS3Bucket
106          THUMB_WIDTH: !Ref ThumbnailWidth
107      Policies:
108        - S3FullAccessPolicy:
109            BucketName: !Ref ThumbnailsS3Bucket
110      Layers:
111        - !GetAtt ImageMagick.Outputs.LayerVersion
```

Invoking system utilities

Now that `mogrify` is available to our Lambda function, we can change the source code for the conversion function to execute it. To start a command line utility from JavaScript, we'll need to use the Node.js child process features. The spawn function from the Node.js `child_process` module uses callbacks. We need to wrap that function into a Promise, so it can be used directly in async functions. (This is a limitation of Node.js, so if you are using a different language, the whole issue with multiple types of asynchronous processes does not apply.) Add another file to your `image-conversion` function directory and call it `child-process-promise.js`. The file should contain the following listing, which is a relatively generic function that will create a subprocess to invoke an external command and print out any console output into the logs so we can troubleshoot more easily.

-------------------- ch10/image-conversion/child-process-promise.js --------------------

```
1  const childProcess = require('child_process');
2  exports.spawn = function (command, argsarray, envoptions) {
3    return new Promise((resolve, reject) => {
4      console.log('executing', command, argsarray.join(' '));
5      const childProc = childProcess.spawn(command, argsarray, envoptions);
```

```
    childProc.stdout.on('data', buffer => console.log(buffer.toString()));
    childProc.stderr.on('data', buffer => console.error(buffer.toString()));
    childProc.on('exit', (code, signal) => {
      console.log(`${command} completed with ${code}:${signal}`);
      if (code || signal) {
        reject(`${command} failed with ${code || signal}`);
      } else {
        resolve();
      }
    });
    childProc.on('error', reject);
  });
};
```

Next, change the index.js file in the image-conversion function directory to include the new child process function, read out the thumbnail width from the environment variables, and run mogrify to process the temporary file. The function should look similar to the code in the following listing (the important changes compared to the code in the previous chapter are lines 8, 9 and 25-28).

──────────────────── ch10/image-conversion/index.js ────────────────────

```
1   const path = require('path'),
2     os = require('os'),
3     s3Util = require('./s3-util'),
4     extractS3Info = require('./extract-s3-info'),
5     silentRemove = require('./silent-remove'),
6     OUTPUT_BUCKET = process.env.OUTPUT_BUCKET,
7     supportedFormats = ['jpg', 'jpeg', 'png', 'gif'],
8     THUMB_WIDTH = process.env.THUMB_WIDTH,
9     childProcessPromise = require('./child-process-promise');
10
11  exports.handler = async (event, context) => {
12    const s3Info = extractS3Info(event),
13      id = context.awsRequestId,
14      extension = path.extname(s3Info.key).toLowerCase(),
15      tempFile = path.join(os.tmpdir(), id + extension),
16      extensionWithoutDot = extension.slice(1),
17      contentType = `image/${extensionWithoutDot}`;
18
19    console.log('converting', s3Info.bucket, ':', s3Info.key, 'using', tempFile);
20
21    if (!supportedFormats.includes(extensionWithoutDot)) {
22      throw new Error(`unsupported file type ${extension}`);
23    }
24    await s3Util.downloadFileFromS3(s3Info.bucket, s3Info.key, tempFile);
25    await childProcessPromise.spawn(
```

```
26      '/opt/bin/mogrify',
27      ['-thumbnail', `${THUMB_WIDTH}x`, tempFile],
28    );
29    await s3Util.uploadFileToS3(OUTPUT_BUCKET, s3Info.key, tempFile, contentType);
30    await silentRemove(tempFile);
31  };
```

To send the new version of the function to the cloud, run sam build and sam package as usual. For deployment, you'll need to activate another CloudFormation feature so it can process nested applications. Add CAPABILITY_AUTO_EXPAND into the list of capabilities:

```
sam deploy --template-file output.yaml --stack-name sam-test-1 --capabilities CAPABILITY_IAM
↪  CAPABILITY_AUTO_EXPAND
```

After SAM has deployed the application, open the main application web page, upload a new image, *wait a few seconds* and then click on the resulting link. You should see the image resized into a 300 pixel wide thumbnail. Don't click on the link immediately, as the result won't be ready instantly. We will address this problem in the next chapter.

Publishing to SAR

In addition to making it easy to use SAR components in our applications, SAM makes it very easy to publish an application directly to the SAR repository. Let's publish our work so far as a private application. We just need to add a bit of metadata about the application to the template. Create a new top-level section called Metadata in template.yaml, with the code similar to the following listing (feel free to change the names).

──────────────────────── ch10/template.yaml ────────────────────────

```
136  Metadata:
137  AWS::ServerlessRepo::Application:
138    Name: image-thumbnails
139    Description: >
140      A sample application for the Running Serverless book tutorial
141    Author: Gojko Adzic
142    SemanticVersion: 1.0.0
143    SpdxLicenseId: MIT
144    LicenseUrl: LICENSE.md
145    ReadmeUrl: README.md
146    Labels: ['layer', 'image', 'lambda', 'imagemagick']
147    HomePageUrl: https://runningserverless.com
148    SourceCodeUrl: https://runningserverless.com
```

Most parameters have obvious purposes. Here is a bit more information about the less obvious parameters:

- SemanticVersion (line 142) is the version of the application. SAR allows you to publish multiple versions of a template, and clients can choose which version to install. Remember that we listed the application ID and the version when including the ImageMagick layer earlier in this chapter.
- SpdxLicenseId (line 143) is the Software Package Data Exchange (SPDX)[6] identifier for the application copyright licence. When uploading private applications you do not need to include a licence, but this is necessary for public applications.
- LicenseUrl (line 144) is also optional for private applications and required for public ones. It points to a file in the function package repository with more information about the usage licence. We'll add it in just a moment.
- ReadmeUrl (line 145) should point to a local file that contains the basic usage instructions for the application. It is also optional for private applications.

Let's create the additional files. You can use markdown to create basic markup such as headers and links. Add a new file to the application directory containing template.yaml, called README.md, containing a description such as in the following listing.

──────────── ch10/README.md ────────────

```
1  A sample application for the Running Serverless book tutorial
```

We also need a licence file. Let's keep it simple. Add a file called LICENSE.md with the following content.

──────────── ch10/LICENSE.md ────────────

```
1  MIT license
```

Before we can publish the application to the repository, we need to allow SAR to read templates from our deployment bucket. Create a file called bucket-policy.json with the content from the following listing (replace BUCKET_NAME in line 10 with the bucket you use to package SAM applications).

──────────── ch10/bucket-policy.json ────────────

```
1  {
2      "Version": "2012-10-17",
3      "Statement": [
4          {
5              "Effect": "Allow",
6              "Principal": {
7                  "Service": "serverlessrepo.amazonaws.com"
8              },
9              "Action": "s3:GetObject",
10             "Resource": "arn:aws:s3:::BUCKET_NAME/*"
11         }
12     ]
13 }
```

Upload this access policy for your bucket to AWS using the following command line:

---

[6] https://spdx.org/licenses/

```
aws s3api put-bucket-policy --bucket BUCKET_NAME --policy fileb://bucket-policy.json
```

Note that you need to do this just once, and SAR will be able to read your bucket in the future. Now build and package the application, but don't deploy it. Instead, use the following command to publish it to SAR:

```
sam publish -t output.yaml
```

In a few moments, you should see the publishing report, showing a link where to check out the application in the repository. Open the link in the browser, and you'll see the information about the published application (Figure 10.2).

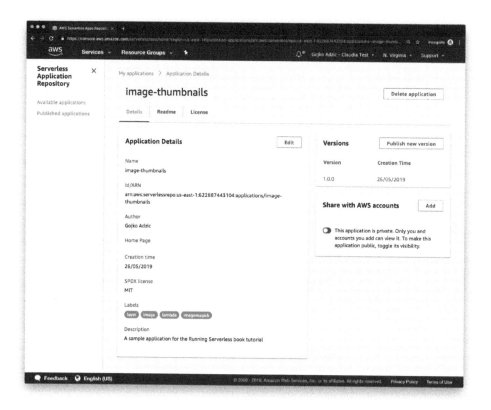

Figure 10.2: *Our new application in the SAR.*

Notice that the menu on the left of Figure 10.2 has two options:

- *Published applications* is the administrative part, allowing you to edit and republish an application. I prefer to use command line tools for that, like we just did.
- *Available applications* is the client-side part, allowing you to browse and deploy existing applications.

Switch to the *Available applications* section then change to the *Private applications* tab (Figure 10.3). Make sure you check the *Show apps that create custom IAM roles* button, and you'll see the application you just published.

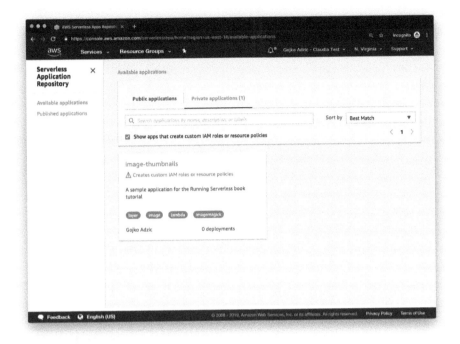

Figure 10.3: *The* Private applications *tab shows your personal applications in the SAR repository.*

Click the title of the application to see the details, and scroll down to the bottom of the page. You will see the application options (Figure 10.4). The repository automatically creates a configuration form for an application using the Parameters section of its SAM template, including custom validation rules and messages. At the very bottom you'll also see a *Deploy* button, which you can use to create a new instance of the application in your account. Of course, deploying from a web page is a bit unnecessary if you have access to the source code of an application, but this is potentially useful for sharing components with external clients.

Using SAR or just sharing templates

CloudFormation templates produced by sam package fully describe a piece of infrastructure, and you can share them with other team members or even publish them on a website so other AWS users can install them. Templates published like that are locked to a particular region, and you'll need to use separate buckets and publish different templates for each available region. Public applications in the SAR are not restricted to a region, so users can easily choose where to deploy them.

After sam publish, the application starts as private, available only to your AWS account. You can share it with other accounts or even make it fully public, using the toggle button in the *Share with AWS accounts* section of the application administrative page (Figure 10.2). If you prefer to use the command line, share a published application by setting its access policy using the aws serverlessrepo command, such as the following one (replace APP_ID with your full application ARN):

```
aws serverlessrepo put-application-policy --application-id APP_ID --statements
↪    Principals='*',Actions=Deploy
```

To share an application with only specific accounts instead of making it public, just list the account principals in the Principals part, instead of using an asterisk.

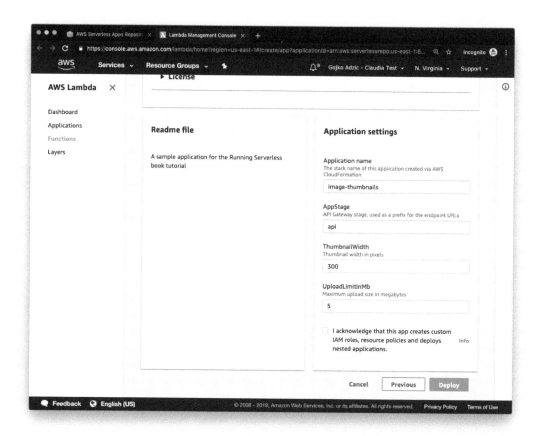

Figure 10.4: *SAR created a configuration form* (Application Settings *on the right side of the page*) *based on the parameters
from our application template.*

Interesting experiments

- Find the ffmpeg layer in the SAR and integrate it into the application. FFMpeg is a popular open-
  source toolkit for video file processing, and you can use it to generate thumbnails from many video
  file formats.
- Create a simple HTTP API backed by a Lambda function, and then share it with a friend or colleague
  using the SAR.

11. Managing sessions and user workflows

This chapter explains how to manage session data in serverless applications and how to reduce operational costs by moving user workflows and application assets out of Lambda functions.

In Chapter 9 we moved resource orchestration from Lambda functions into the AWS platform. This significantly reduced operational costs, but we can do even better. In fact, we can halve the costs for running our application by moving another coordination piece out of Lambda, this time related to user workflows. In the process, we can also make the application much more robust and user friendly.

Up until this chapter, we used Lambda functions to generate HTML code for browsers. For example, once a user has uploaded a file, S3 will redirect them to the /confirm URL. This API resource is connected to the ConfirmUploadFunction, which will generate a download link for the results. The function will actually send a full HTML page, including the download link, back to the client so their browser can display it. This is simple and convenient for explaining the basic concepts, but it is far from ideal. There are three big problems with the current state of the application, mostly caused by the implicit relationship between uploads and downloads.

The first problem is that there is no feedback from the conversion process to the client. We generate the result link in the upload confirmation page. S3 triggers the Lambda function for file conversions around the same time as when it redirects users to the confirmation page, so it's anybody's guess what will happen first. This is why I suggested waiting a few seconds before clicking the link in the previous chapter. The result link must not appear before the result is ready, or someone might click it while the conversion is still running and think that the application is broken. If we knew the duration of the conversion process, we could delay displaying the link on the client side. Without a good feedback mechanism, it's very difficult to guess the duration.

The second problem is that there is no error handling. If something explodes in the background, the clients will never know about it. If an image takes a long time to convert, users won't know whether the process has stopped due to an error or due to a timeout on the server, or whether it's still running.

The third problem is that we have two Lambda functions that share an implicit session state, represented by the uploaded file key. ConfirmUploadFunction generates the download link based on the file key from the redirect request, configured in ShowFormFunction. This is not really secure, because someone might modify the URL parameters and try to access a different file. We used GUIDs, so it's reasonably difficult to guess key identifiers. We need to make this implicit state significantly more secure.

All three problems require a much more explicit workflow and some sensible way of keeping session state. The typical solution in a traditional web application would be to handle the user session workflow in the middle application layer. But with serverless architectures, keeping the user session workflows in the application layer can create all sorts of subtle problems.

Website clusters usually work by sending all requests from a single user to the same machine so that web servers can keep session state in memory. With Lambda, application developers do not control request routing, so sticky sessions are not possible. Requests from the same user might reach two different Lambda instances with different memory session states.

Request routing is one of the least intuitive aspects of serverless applications for people used to web servers. There are many nice tools that make it easy to repackage classic server web applications into Lambda functions. For example, aws-serverless-express[1] makes it possible to deploy existing Express applications as Lambda functions with minimal modifications. But beware that if such applications are based on server-side sessions, this is just looking for trouble. The application might work perfectly fine during testing, because the load might not reach the threshold for Lambda to start more than one instance. However, once

---

[1]https://github.com/awslabs/aws-serverless-express

real user traffic starts hitting multiple containers at the same time, the application will mysteriously experience problems.

Moving session state out of Lambda functions

Regardless of the application architecture, session state can't reside in Lambda functions; it has to go somewhere else.

The usual solution for fault-tolerant session state in three-tier applications would be to put it into some kind of distributed data grid. DynamoDB would fit well in this case. Each Lambda instance could read out the session state at the beginning of a request, and save it towards the end. This would make each function slower and increase the operational cost of the application significantly. It would also make the application more error prone, since a function might experience problems between updating session state and returning the result to the client.

There is an alternative that makes the application significantly cheaper. In Chapter 8, we moved the gatekeeper responsibility out of the application business code layer to the platform. As a result, client code can talk directly to AWS resources using temporary access grants. Service resources (such as S3) can directly prevent the client from performing something it is not authorised to do. Keeping the workflow on the server side is not really improving security. This means it is safe to move user workflows all the way to the client devices, and with them, move user session data as well. Instead of trying to make the back end stateful, we can keep the user state on the front end.

If the client code is under your control, with serverless applications it's usually best to move user workflows and sessions to the client layer. This can significantly reduce operational costs and increase overall performance. You do not have to pay for Lambda functions waiting on resources, polling and coordinating work. Client devices will take that responsibility and that cost. Although the overall application data will be distributed across many different client devices, the session state of each individual user will be in a single place (the client device). This approach makes it easy to avoid all sorts of problems typically related to distributed data, and ensure consistency.

If someone else controls the client code, for example if you are building a Slack integration or a Facebook messenger chatbot, put session state in DynamoDB.

Resumable sessions

A big limitation of moving session state to client devices is that unexpected problems on the front end can cause users to lose session information. If the browser crashes half-way through a workflow, the client will not be able to resume the session. For our image thumbnail application, this is not an issue. The client can just re-request another upload policy and try again.

If you want to create resumable sessions or let users access the same workflow from multiple browser tabs or even devices concurrently, then you'll need to synchronise session state somehow. In typical three-tier architectures, the solution for that would be to keep the session in the application server or in a database. With serverless applications, there are several ways of synchronising client sessions without the application layer:

- Amazon Cognito has its own synchronisation mechanism for a small amount of user data such as preferences. It's called Cognito Sync[2].
- For more complex objects, you can give clients direct access to a DynamoDB table, where each user is restricted to reading and writing only their state.
- For situations where different users need to share session state (for example in collaborative editing), use AWS AppSync[3]. AWS AppSync is a managed hierarchical database intended for direct use by client devices, and it can automatically synchronise state across multiple clients, resolve conflicts, and even deal with offline usage scenarios.

Of course, all three approaches work well with Lambda functions, and you can add triggers to act on changes to data from the server side.

Minimise coordination

With state on the client, we need to minimise the chatter between the client devices and network services, and the amount of coordination between different Lambda executions. There are two ways to achieve this:

- For tightly coupled tasks, aggregate processing so that different requests are independent.
- For loosely coupled tasks, send full context information with each request.

The two Lambda functions we created in the previous chapter are quite tightly coupled. In order to securely generate the download link, we need to know the file key from the upload policy. With such a tight coupling, it's better to aggregate the processing.

The ShowFormFunction Lambda function should create both the upload policy and the download signature. That is the easiest way to ensure that users can only download conversion results for their own files. That function does not, however, need to produce HTML code. There is no need to coordinate the formatting of a web form between the client device and a Lambda function. User interface formatting can safely move to client devices, without any security risks. We can simplify the Lambda function by making it return the security grants in a simple format that a client device can understand, for example as a JSON object. Software running on the client side can then create the appropriate user interface. This would also allow us to create a nicer front end by using a popular front-end framework such as React or Angular, without complicating the Lambda code.

Generating both security signatures in ShowFormFunction means that we can completely remove the ConfirmUploadFunction function and reduce the operational costs by avoiding one Lambda execution and one API call for each upload. This will almost halve the operational costs for the application. We will not use redirects after uploading any more, because the fact that the upload finished is not really that important. The client code needs to know when the conversion finished, closing the whole feedback loop, in order to show the download link only after the actual result is available.

---

[2]https://docs.aws.amazon.com/cognito/latest/developerguide/cognito-sync.html
[3]https://aws.amazon.com/appsync/

Controlling the user sessions from client side will allow us to create a much better end-user experience and reduce operational costs. The downside is that the client code will need to be more complex, and we will need some way of deploying and managing web assets and client-side code in addition to Lambda code.

Moving static assets out of Lambda functions

Traditional web applications bundle code and assets, and web servers are responsible for sending both to client devices. Translated to the Lambda world, that would mean including client-side JavaScript and web assets in a Lambda function, and creating at least another API endpoint and a new function to send those files to clients on demand.

Serving application contents such as images, style sheets, client-side JavaScript and HTML files through a Lambda function is a bad idea. Those files are typically public and require no authorisation. They do not change depending on individual users or requests. Paying for a Lambda function and an API call for every file request would increase operational costs significantly and introduce two unnecessary intermediaries between the user and file contents, increasing latency and degrading the user experience.

With serverless applications, it's much more usual to put static assets somewhere for clients to fetch them directly, for example on S3. In fact, this is so common that S3 can pretend to be a web server. It even offers some basic web serving features out of the box, such as redirects and customising response headers. Browsers can directly load files from S3 using HTTPS.

In the previous chapters, we uploaded private files to S3 and generated temporary security grants for browsers to download them. We can also upload public files, and client devices will be able to access them without a particular temporary grant. There will be no need to involve a Lambda function in the process at all. That way, we only need to pay for data transfer for static assets. This is significantly cheaper then adding another API call and a function execution. Users will also get faster responses. It will be better for everyone.

Use a content distribution network

For high-traffic applications, it's usual to put a content distribution network (CDN) between users and S3 files, making the application even faster. AWS has a CDN called CloudFront, which can cache static files from S3 all over the world and even compress them automatically before sending them to users. CloudFront can also run Lambda functions to perform some quick business logic such as transforming responses or modifying incoming or outgoing headers. For our simple application, this would be unnecessary, so we'll just use S3 directly.

Let's restructure the application to look as in Figure 11.1. The client can load static assets directly from S3 without going through Lambda. A single API operation should send back both upload and download signatures, and client code can take over the remaining coordination tasks.

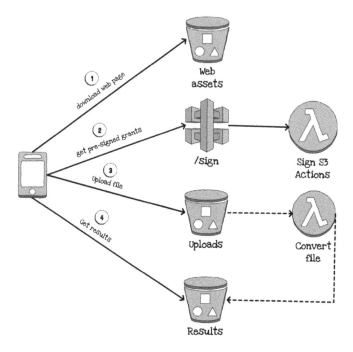

Figure 11.1: *User workflow and session data will move to the client layer, making the application infrastructure significantly cheaper.*

Create a sub-directory called web-site in the project directory (app), and inside it create create a file called user-workflow.js. This file will contain the whole client-side JavaScript code. For a more complex application, it would be better to split code up into individual files and somehow post-process it (for example using webpack), but client-side code packaging is outside the scope of this book.

First, we'll need a utility function that can retrieve an object with combined signatures for uploading and downloading, given an API URL. We'll use the HTML5 fetch function and parse the result as a JSON object. Add the code from the following listing to user-workflow.js.

———————————————————— ch11/web-site/user-workflow.js ————————————————————

```
async function getSignatures(apiUrl) {
  if (!apiUrl) {
    throw 'Please provide an API URL';
  }
  const response = await fetch(apiUrl);
  return response.json();
};
```

In order to upload files and handle errors gracefully in a single web page, we can't let users upload a file with a browser form submission, because that causes a page reload. We'll need a utility function to submit form data in the background using an asynchronous network request. In this case, we won't use fetch but the older XMLHttpRequest interface. Users will be uploading large files, and fetch does not notify callers about progress. Using XMLHttpRequest will allow us to visually show updates during an upload. Add the following function to user-workflow.js.

ch11/web-site/user-workflow.js

```
function postFormData(url, formData, progress) {
  return new Promise((resolve, reject) => {
    const request = new XMLHttpRequest();
    const sendError = (e, label) => {
      console.error(e);
      reject(label);
    };
    request.open('POST', url);
    request.upload.addEventListener('error', e =>
      sendError(e, 'upload error')
    );
    request.upload.addEventListener('timeout', e =>
      sendError(e, 'upload timeout')
    );
    request.upload.addEventListener('progress', progress);
    request.addEventListener('load', () => {
      if (request.status ≥ 200 && request.status < 400) {
        resolve();
      } else {
        reject(request.responseText);
      }
    });
    request.addEventListener('error', e =>
      sendError(e, 'server error')
    );
    request.addEventListener('abort', e =>
      sendError(e, 'server aborted request')
    );
    request.send(formData);
  });
};
```

If users try uploading a file that is too large, or if the policy expires, S3 will respond with an XML status. We'll need a small utility function to parse the XML response and get the actual error out. Add the following function to user-workflow.js.

─────────────────────── ch11/web-site/user-workflow.js ───────────────────────

```
39  function parseXML(xmlString, textQueryElement) {
40    const parser = new DOMParser(),
41      doc = parser.parseFromString(xmlString, 'application/xml'),
42      element = textQueryElement && doc.querySelector(textQueryElement);
43    if (!textQueryElement) {
44      return doc;
45    }
46    return element && element.textContent;
47  };
```

The client code will need to simulate submitting a web form with a file. Browsers will let us access the contents of an input form field containing a file object as a Blob, and we can just post that using a standard browser FileData object. Add the following function to user-workflow.js.

─────────────────────── ch11/web-site/user-workflow.js ───────────────────────

```
48  function uploadBlob(uploadPolicy, fileBlob, progress) {
49    const formData = new window.FormData();
50    Object.keys(uploadPolicy.fields).forEach((key) =>
51      formData.append(key, uploadPolicy.fields[key])
52    );
53    formData.append('file', fileBlob);
54    return postFormData(uploadPolicy.url, formData, progress)
55      .catch(e => {
56        if (parseXML(e, 'Code') === 'EntityTooLarge') {
57          throw `File ${fileBlob.name} is too big to upload.`;
58        };
59        throw 'server error';
60      });
61  };
```

The user workflow function should periodically check whether the conversion Lambda has finished the job and let users know when the resulting file is ready to download. S3 supports partial requests by using the Range header. That enables us to try downloading only a small part of the resulting file (for example the first 10 bytes), to check if the file exists. Add the following two functions to user-workflow.js.

─────────────────────── ch11/web-site/user-workflow.js ───────────────────────

```
62  function promiseTimeout(timeout) {
63    return new Promise(resolve => {
64      setTimeout(resolve, timeout);
65    });
66  };
67  async function pollForResult(url, timeout, times) {
68    if (times <= 0) {
69      throw 'no retries left';
```

```
     }
     await promiseTimeout(timeout);
     try {
       const response = await fetch(url, {
         method: 'GET',
         mode: 'cors',
         headers: {
           'Range': 'bytes=0-10'
         }
       });
       if (!response.ok) {
         console.log('file not ready, retrying');
         return pollForResult(url, timeout, times - 1);
       }
       return 'OK';
     } catch (e) {
       console.error('network error');
       console.error(e);
       return pollForResult(url, timeout, times - 1);
     }
   };
```

S3 HeadObject requests

S3 also supports a HeadObject request that retrieves object metadata. We could have used that instead of trying to download the first 10 bytes to check for a file. That would require generating another signature in Lambda for the HeadObject operation, and we don't really care about metadata in this case, so it is simpler to just request some initial bytes to check whether a file exists.

Next, we can start composing the visual part of the workflow. First, let's create a simple web page that will let us show different steps of the workflow. The web page also needs to load the client application JavaScript from an external file. Create a new file called index.html in the web-site directory, with the content similar to the following listing.

———————————— ch11/web-site/index.html ————————————

```
<html>
  <body>
    <div step="initial">
      <h1>Select a file</h1>
      <input type="hidden" id="apiurl" value="${API_URL}" />
      <input type="file" id="picker"/>
    </div>
    <div step="uploading" style="display: none">
```

```
 9        Please wait, uploading...
10        <br/>
11        <progress id="progressbar" max="100" value="0" />
12      </div>
13      <div step="converting" style="display: none">
14        Please wait, converting your file...
15      </div>
16      <div step="result" style="display: none">
17        <h1>Your thumbnail is ready</h1>
18        <a id="resultlink">download it</a>
19      </div>
20      <div step="error" style="display: none">
21        <h1>There was an error creating the thumbnail</h1>
22        <p id="errortext"></p>
23      </div>
24      <script src="user-workflow.js"></script>
25    </body>
26  </html>
```

Notice the placeholder for the API URL on line 5 of the previous listing. In earlier chapters, we just used a relative URL for the upload form. We could do that because both the form and the processing endpoint were in the same API, so they were under the same web domain. After we have introduced the changes in this chapter, client devices will download the web assets (including the index.html file we just created) from S3, but they will need to upload the files to our API Gateway, which will be on a different domain. We need to somehow let the client device know about the API Gateway URL. In theory, you could use the actual value of your API endpoint URL directly in the file, but that would make it difficult to deploy different versions for development, testing and production from the same source. Instead, we'll use a placeholder value here and replace it with the actual URL during deployment.

To change the web page according to the workflow steps, we'll need a utility function that can show a named section of the page and hide all the other sections. The sections of our index.html page have a custom HTML attribute called step that we can use for this purpose. Add the following function to user-workflow.js.

───────────────────── ch11/web-site/user-workflow.js ─────────────────────

```
 91  function showStep(label) {
 92    const sections = Array.from(document.querySelectorAll('[step]'));
 93    sections.forEach(section => {
 94      if (section.getAttribute('step') === label) {
 95        section.style.display = '';
 96      } else {
 97        section.style.display = 'none';
 98      }
 99    });
100  };
```

We will also want to display a progress bar during uploads. The standard XMLHttpRequest progress event contains two fields, total and loaded, containing the number of bytes that are expected to transfer and the number of bytes transferred so far. We'll populate a HTML5 progress element, which has two corresponding attributes, max and value. Add the following function to user-workflow.js.

―――――――――――――――――――――― ch11/web-site/user-workflow.js ――――――――――――――――――――――

```
1  function progressNotifier(progressEvent) {
2    const progressElement = document.getElementById('progressbar');
3    const total = progressEvent.total;
4    const current = progressEvent.loaded;
5    if (current && total) {
6      progressElement.setAttribute('max', total);
7      progressElement.setAttribute('value', current);
8    }
9  };
```

We now have all the pieces to compose a thumbnail conversion workflow. We can wait for users to select a file, then show the progress message and upload the Blob, wait for the conversion results, and then show the download link. In case of any trouble, we can show the error message. Add the following function to user-workflow.js.

―――――――――――――――――――――― ch11/web-site/user-workflow.js ――――――――――――――――――――――

```
10  async function startUpload(evt) {
11    const picker = evt.target;
12    const file = picker.files && picker.files[0];
13    const apiUrl = document.getElementById('apiurl').value;
14
15    if (file && file.name) {
16      picker.value = '';
17      try {
18        showStep('uploading');
19        const signatures = await getSignatures(apiUrl);
20        console.log('got signatures', signatures);
21        await uploadBlob(signatures.upload, file, progressNotifier);
22        showStep('converting');
23        await pollForResult(signatures.download, 3000, 20);
24        const downloadLink = document.getElementById('resultlink');
25        downloadLink.setAttribute('href', signatures.download);
26        showStep('result');
27      } catch (e) {
28        console.error(e);
29        const displayError = e.message || JSON.stringify(e);
30        document.getElementById('errortext').innerHTML = displayError;
31        showStep('error');
32      }
```

```
133      }
134    };
```

Lastly, something has to start the workflow method when a user selects a file. Let's add a bit of code to the web page initialisation that calls the startUpload function when the file picker state changes. Add the following function to user-workflow.js.

─────────────────────────── ch11/web-site/user-workflow.js ───────────────────────────

```
135    function initPage() {
136      const picker = document.getElementById('picker');
137      showStep('initial');
138      picker.addEventListener('change', startUpload);
139    };
140    window.addEventListener('DOMContentLoaded', initPage);
```

Using S3 as a web server

There are two ways of using S3 as a web server: bucket endpoints and website endpoints.

A *bucket endpoint* allows direct access to S3 objects using HTTPS. AWS automatically activates this endpoint when a you create an S3 bucket. For example, a file called test.txt in the bucket gojko will be available from https://gojko.s3.amazonaws.com/test.txt. Access to the bucket endpoint is controlled by IAM. When uploading a file to S3, you can make it publicly readable (as I did with test.txt), so anyone can access it using a web browser. You can also mark the file as private, so others will need a pre-signed download policy to access it. We used this approach for conversion results in the previous chapter.

A *website endpoint* is an optional feature of S3 that can perform some basic web workflows, such as redirecting users or showing index or error pages. This endpoint has a different URL from the bucket endpoint, usually a subdomain of s3-website-us-east-1.amazonaws.com in the us-east-1 region, or a similar service for other regions. To use a website endpoint, you need to activate it after creating the bucket. You can activate a website endpoint for an S3 bucket from the AWS Web Console, using the *Static web site hosting* section of the bucket properties page. Of course, it's possible to activate it using CloudFormation as well, using the WebsiteConfiguration properties of a bucket.

Set a custom domain name

S3 will automatically assign a domain name to a website endpoint. It's not possible to set a custom domain name, but you can put a CDN between the users and the website endpoint and configure a custom domain name in the CDN. This is the usual approach for creating nice web domains for serverless applications.

Requests for the bucket endpoint only work with URLs matching an exact resource path, so asking for the root object (/) will not automatically show index.html. We can set up the website endpoint to send back an index file if users ask for the root object.

Another major difference between website endpoints and bucket endpoints is that website endpoints work using HTTP, while bucket endpoints work using HTTPS. This might sound like a security problem, but for real-world production usage I always put a content distribution network in front of the S3 website endpoint, so the CDN provides HTTPS access to users. If you use Amazon's CDN, then the CDN talks to the S3 website endpoint only internally in the AWS network, so the risk of man-in-the-middle attacks between the CDN and the origin isn't that big.

We'll need another bucket to host the files from our web-site directory. Users will expect to see a landing page when they type a domain in their web browsers, so let's create a new S3 bucket for static assets and set up a website endpoint. Add another resource to the Resources section on the template, with the code from the following listing (indented so that WebAssetsS3Bucket aligns with other resource names, such as UploadS3Bucket).

—————————— ch11/template.yaml ——————————

```
26  WebAssetsS3Bucket:
27    Type: AWS::S3::Bucket
28    Properties:
29      WebsiteConfiguration:
30        ErrorDocument: 404.html
31        IndexDocument: index.html
```

Notice the two files referenced in lines 30 and 31. That is how the website endpoint knows how to respond to root object requests and what to send back in case of missing files. We already have the index file, so let's add a simple error page to our web-site directory. Call it 404.html.

—————————— ch11/web-site/404.html ——————————

```
1  <html>
2    <body>
3      <h1>Page not found</h1>
4    </body>
5  </html>
```

When you configure a website endpoint for a bucket, AWS creates a separate website URL, which you can access in the SAM template using the WebsiteURL property. To be able to discover the website after we deploy the application, let's create another output in the application template. Add the code from the following listing to the Outputs section of your template, indented so that WebUrl aligns with other outputs.

—————————— ch11/template.yaml ——————————

```
177  WebUrl:
178    Description: "Public web URL"
179    Value: !GetAtt WebAssetsS3Bucket.WebsiteURL
```

Working with cross-origin resource sharing

Client code will need to access resources from S3 and API Gateway, which will be on different domains. To prevent online fraud, browsers request special authorisation when a page from one domain wants to access resources on another domain. This is cross-origin resource sharing (CORS). Here's a quick introduction to how CORS works that will be enough for our needs (for a more in-depth introduction to CORS, check out the *Cross-Origin Resource Sharing*[4] documentation page on the Mozilla Developer Network):

An *origin*, in browser terminology, is a combination of URL protocol, domain and, optionally, network port. So, for example, the origin https://runningserverless.com is distinct from https://gojko.net. Browsers will happily load scripts or images from a different origin during primary web page parsing, but they will not allow background network requests to different origins so willingly. For example, a page from runningserverless.com can include an image from gojko.net in its HTML contents without any special configuration. However, the same page will not be able to read the same image asynchronously using JavaScript unless the CORS settings of gojko.net explicitly allow it.

Before executing a network request from JavaScript code, browsers will verify that the page is actually allowed to access a resource on a different origin. Browsers do that by sending a *pre-flight* request to the resource URL. The pre-flight request is an HTTP call using the *OPTIONS* method, including the resource it wants to access and the CORS context URL. It's essentially a browser asking the remote server: 'If I were to try making this request for a page from this origin, would you let me?'

The resource server is supposed to reply to the pre-flight request repeating the requested origin and providing a list of HTTP headers and methods it would allow for that resource. Technically, the server response needs to include the policy in the `Access-Control-Allow-Origin`, `Access-Control-Allow-Methods` and `Access-Control-Allow-Headers` HTTP headers.

The browser then compares the allowed methods and headers to the request the JavaScript code wants to send. If everything matches, it proceeds with the full request. Otherwise, it will make the JavaScript code think that there was a network error.

When the resource server responds to the full request (not just the pre-flight request), it also needs to include the *Access-Control-Allow-Origin* header, responding with the same origin as the current page. Without that, the browser will refuse to pass the result back to the JavaScript code.

> CORS security errors are particularly tricky to troubleshoot, because they only apply to background browser actions. Running exactly the same request from a command line, for example using curl, won't show any problems. You won't find any logs on the server about such problems, because browsers kill requests before they even reach your API.

When we move web assets to a separate website endpoint and move the client workflows to JavaScript, we'll introduce potential CORS issues into the application.

The first step in Figure 11.1, retrieving the web page, is a direct request, so it falls outside CORS.

---

[4]https://developer.mozilla.org/en-US/docs/Web/HTTP/CORS

The second step ('get pre-signed grants') will be a JavaScript call to the API Gateway URL, which will be on a different origin, so it will be restricted by CORS.

The third step ('upload file') will post a form dynamically to the uploads bucket URL, also on a different origin and restricted by CORS.

The fourth step ('get results') also requires CORS, because we'll be polling the results bucket dynamically to check whether the file is ready.

Configuring S3 buckets for CORS

The second and third CORS issues are easy to address. Because S3 supports basic web serving features, including CORS, we can use CloudFormation to configure CORS policies on S3 buckets. We just need to add the CORS origin (the website endpoint for the static assets) to the upload and thumbnails bucket using the `CorsConfiguration` property.

The upload bucket should only allow POST requests across origins, and only from the pages loaded from the assets bucket. Change the `UploadS3Bucket` resource in your template to match the following listing (the important changes are in lines 39-47).

—————————————— ch11/template.yaml ——————————————

```
32  UploadS3Bucket:
33    Type: AWS::S3::Bucket
34    Properties:
35      BucketEncryption:
36        ServerSideEncryptionConfiguration:
37          - ServerSideEncryptionByDefault:
38              SSEAlgorithm: AES256
39      CorsConfiguration:
40        CorsRules:
41          - AllowedHeaders:
42              - "*"
43            AllowedMethods:
44              - POST
45            AllowedOrigins:
46              - !GetAtt WebAssetsS3Bucket.WebsiteURL
47            MaxAge: 3600
```

The results bucket should only allow GET requests across origins, from the pages loaded from the web assets bucket. Change the `ThumbnailsS3Bucket` resource in your application template to match the following listing (the important changes are in lines 55-63).

—————————————— ch11/template.yaml ——————————————

```
48  ThumbnailsS3Bucket:
49    Type: AWS::S3::Bucket
```

```
50    Properties:
51      BucketEncryption:
52        ServerSideEncryptionConfiguration:
53          - ServerSideEncryptionByDefault:
54              SSEAlgorithm: AES256
55      CorsConfiguration:
56        CorsRules:
57          - AllowedHeaders:
58              - "*"
59            AllowedMethods:
60              - GET
61            AllowedOrigins:
62              - !GetAtt WebAssetsS3Bucket.WebsiteURL
63            MaxAge: 3600
```

For more information on the `CorsRules` setting and the `WebsiteURL` property of the S3 bucket resource, check out the AWS::S3::Bucket[5] documentation page.

Configuring API Gateway for CORS

The CORS request going from the web page to our API is going to be a bit more tricky. We'll need to add an `OPTIONS` handler to the API and also change the response in our function to include the correct origin.

There are two ways of configuring `OPTIONS` handlers. The first is to add a Lambda function and an API endpoint. This would make it fully flexible, so we could dynamically calculate the right origin and response headers, but it would add an API call and a Lambda execution to our costs. In cases where we don't really need a dynamic response, such as where we always have a single valid origin, we could also just configure a static response in the API Gateway. This requires no backing Lambda, so it is cheaper but less flexible.

SAM has a nice shortcut for configuring a static response. Just add a `Cors` property to the API resource, with the supported origin. Note that this uses a slightly overcomplicated syntax. API Gateway needs quotes around header values, so we'll need to wrap the website URL in quotes using CloudFormation string substitution. Change the API definition in your application template to match the following listing (the important addition is in line 68).

─────────────────────── ch11/template.yaml ───────────────────────

```
64  WebApi:
65    Type: AWS::Serverless::Api
66    Properties:
67      StageName: !Ref AppStage
68      Cors: !Sub "'${WebAssetsS3Bucket.WebsiteURL}'"
```

---

[5]https://docs.aws.amazon.com/AWSCloudFormation/latest/UserGuide/aws-properties-s3-bucket.html

You can set individual CORS properties such as allowed headers or caching by providing an object instead of just a simple URL. Check out the *Cors Configuration*[6] section of the AWS SAM API resource for more information.

The API Cors property is enough to handle pre-flight requests, but the response from ShowFormFunction will also need to send the CORS origin header back to the client browser. We'll need to let the function know about the allowed origin using another environment variable, for example named CORS_ORIGIN.

Because we're switching from HTML over to JSON, add another file to your user-form function directory to format JSON responses. The file should be called json-response.js and contain the code from the following listing. It will append the allowed CORS origin to all responses.

──────────────── ch11/user-form/json-response.js ────────────────

```
1  module.exports = function jsonResponse(body) {
2    return {
3      statusCode: 200,
4      body: JSON.stringify(body),
5      headers: {
6        'Content-Type': 'application/json',
7        'Access-Control-Allow-Origin': process.env.CORS_ORIGIN
8      }
9    };
10  };
```

We can now modify the ShowFormFunction code to generate both the upload policy and the download signature and send everything back wrapped into a JSON response. To do that, the function also needs to know about the output bucket, so we'll need to configure another environment variable later, for example THUMB-NAILS_S3_BUCKET. Change the show-form.js function code in the user-form directory to match the following listing.

──────────────── ch11/user-form/show-form.js ────────────────

```
1  const jsonResponse = require('./json-response');
2  const aws = require('aws-sdk');
3  const s3 = new aws.S3();
4  const uploadLimitInMB = parseInt(process.env.UPLOAD_LIMIT_IN_MB);
5  exports.lambdaHandler = async (event, context) => {
6    const key = context.awsRequestId + '.jpg',
7      uploadParams = {
8        Bucket: process.env.UPLOAD_S3_BUCKET,
9        Expires: 600,
10        Conditions: [
11          ['content-length-range', 1, uploadLimitInMB * 1000000]
12        ],
13        Fields: {
14          acl: 'private',
```

───────────────────────

[6]https://github.com/awslabs/serverless-application-model/blob/master/versions/2016-10-31.md#cors-configuration

```
15          key: key
16        }
17      },
18      uploadForm = s3.createPresignedPost(uploadParams),
19      downloadParams = {
20        Bucket: process.env.THUMBNAILS_S3_BUCKET,
21        Key: key,
22        Expires: 600
23      },
24      downloadUrl = s3.getSignedUrl('getObject', downloadParams);
25    return jsonResponse({
26      upload: uploadForm,
27      download: downloadUrl
28    });
29  };
```

Lastly, we need to modify the ShowFormFunction configuration in the SAM template to add the new environment variables and to let it read from the output bucket. Although the function itself will never read from the output bucket, it will need the permission to do so. Remember that IAM signatures can never pass on grants that the signing key does not already have. Modify the ShowFormFunction template configuration to match the following listing (the important changes are in lines 86, 87 and 91-92).

─────────────────────────── ch11/template.yaml ───────────────────────────

```
69  ShowFormFunction:
70    Type: AWS::Serverless::Function
71    Properties:
72      CodeUri: user-form/
73      Handler: show-form.lambdaHandler
74      Runtime: nodejs12.x
75      Events:
76        ShowForm:
77          Type: Api
78          Properties:
79            Path: /
80            Method: get
81            RestApiId: !Ref WebApi
82      Environment:
83        Variables:
84          UPLOAD_S3_BUCKET: !Ref UploadS3Bucket
85          UPLOAD_LIMIT_IN_MB: !Ref UploadLimitInMb
86          CORS_ORIGIN: !GetAtt WebAssetsS3Bucket.WebsiteURL
87          THUMBNAILS_S3_BUCKET: !Ref ThumbnailsS3Bucket
88      Policies:
89        - S3FullAccessPolicy:
90            BucketName: !Ref UploadS3Bucket
```

```
  - S3ReadPolicy:
      BucketName: !Ref ThumbnailsS3Bucket
```

The `ConfirmUploadFunction` is now obsolete, so you can delete that resource from the application template, and the related source code files.

Uploading files to S3

We added a `web-site` directory to our project, with static web assets. Before we can deploy the new version of the application, we need to send those assets to S3 and replace the placeholder for the API URL in the index file.

At the time when I wrote this, CloudFormation didn't have any built-in support for sending web asset files to S3. However, there is a component in the AWS Serverless Application Repository that can handle simple uploads to S3, which is just what we need to deploy everything at the same time. `DeployToS3`[7], created by Aleksandar Simović, can upload files to S3 and optionally replace patterns in those files with CloudFormation references. That component will make it very easy to coordinate API Gateway updates and static website assets. Import the component into the application template by adding it to the Resources section. Add the code from the following listing, indented so it aligns with existing resources (for example `Convert-FileFunction`).

——————————— ch11/template.yaml ———————————

```
6  DeployToS3:
87   Type: AWS::Serverless::Application
88   Properties:
89     Location:
.0      ApplicationId: arn:aws:serverlessrepo:us-east-1:375983427419:applications/deploy-to-s3
41      SemanticVersion: 1.0.0
```

CloudFormation and SAM can only package files from a local directory for Lambda functions. `DeployToS3` slightly abuses the Lambda packaging process to trick CloudFormation into collecting files from a local directory with web assets and uploading them to S3.

In order for CloudFormation to package the `web-site` directory files, we need to make it think it's collecting the source code for a Lambda function. For that, we just need to create another `AWS::Serverless:Function` resource and point it to the local directory. That function, of course, won't be able to run, because it does not contain executable code or a Lambda handler. Also, the files will be, in that case, deployed to a Lambda container, not to S3. That's where the `DeployToS3` component comes in. It contains a Lambda layer with a Python function handler. When we attach the layer to the fake Lambda function, it will make the function executable. Once the handler from the layer runs, it uploads the current function source code (which will be the contents of the `web-site` directory) to a specified S3 location.

---

[7]https://serverlessrepo.aws.amazon.com/applications/arn:aws:serverlessrepo:us-east-1:375983427419:applications~deploy-to-s3

The `Arn` output of the `DeployToS3` component will contain the layer reference, so we'll need to add that to the fake function. We'll also need to ensure that the function can write to the web assets bucket, so that the handler from the layer can upload the files. Add the block from the following listing to the `Resources` section of your template, aligned with the `DeployToS3` resource.

─────────────────────────────────── ch11/template.yaml ───────────────────────────────────

```
142  SiteSource:
143    Type: AWS::Serverless::Function
144    Properties:
145      Layers:
146        - !GetAtt DeployToS3.Outputs.Arn
147      CodeUri: web-site/
148      AutoPublishAlias: production
149      Runtime: python3.7
150      Handler: deployer.resource_handler
151      Timeout: 600
152      Policies:
153        - S3FullAccessPolicy:
154            BucketName: !Ref WebAssetsS3Bucket
```

The layer works as a Python application, and lines 149 and 150 configure the function so that the layer can take over the execution. This allows us to deploy web assets without developing any new code, and by packaging the Lambda function just with the website assets.

Line 149 from the previous listing is very important. The handler in the `DeployToS3` layer is written in Python and supports Python 3.6 and 3.7 Lambda environments. SAM will try to build all local functions when we run `sam build`, including the fake function, so change this configuration line to match your local Python version. If you don't do that, SAM will complain about a Python binary mismatch.

> At the time when I wrote this, `sam build` for Python applications failed unless the function directory contained a package manifest file, even if it had no dependencies. Create an empty file called `requirements.txt` in the `web-site` directory to trick it into packaging up the assets.

Using custom resources to extend CloudFormation

CloudFormation will now package the `web-site` directory files with our template. It will also create the `Site-Source` Lambda function containing those files. We now just need to make the Lambda function execute during deployments, instead of waiting for someone to manually trigger it later. CloudFormation can do that with a feature called *custom resource*.

Custom resources are extensions to CloudFormation, handling application-specific workflows that are not supported by standard components, such as uploading files to S3. When declaring a custom resource, we can tell CloudFormation to execute a Lambda function, which is ideal for the SiteSource fake function. In fact, the layer created by DeployToS3 is intended to work this way, so it supports the custom resource workflow out of the box.

To declare a custom resource, just add another block to the Resources section of the template, using the type AWS::CloudFormation::CustomResource. Custom resources require one property, named ServiceToken, pointing to a Lambda function that CloudFormation needs to execute. You can add any other properties required for the resource to function.

To run the SiteSource function during deployment, we need to create a custom resource with the function ARN as the ServiceToken. We will also need to configure a few other properties required by the DeployToS3 component:

- TargetBucket should point to an S3 bucket for file uploads.
- Acl is an optional property defining the access control for uploaded files. We want to serve public files but not let anyone change them, so we'll need to specify public-read.
- CacheControlMaxAge sets the optional browser caching period in seconds. For static files, we can safely turn on caching.
- Substitutions is an optional property containing two fields: FilePattern is a regular expression that tells DeployToS3 which files to search for placeholders, and Values maps placeholder names to replacements. We changed index.html to include a placeholder for the API_URL, so we can now define the appropriate substitution.

Add the block from the following listing to the Resources section of your template, aligned with the Site-Source resource.

──────────────── ch11/template.yaml ────────────────

```
155  DeploymentResource:
156    Type: AWS::CloudFormation::CustomResource
157    Properties:
158      ServiceToken: !GetAtt SiteSource.Arn
159      Version: !Ref "SiteSource.Version"
160      TargetBucket: !Ref WebAssetsS3Bucket
161      Substitutions:
162        FilePattern: "*.html"
163        Values:
164          API_URL: !Sub "https://${WebApi}.execute-api.${AWS::Region}.amazonaws.com/${AppStage}/"
165      Acl: 'public-read'
166      CacheControlMaxAge: 600
```

Redeploying custom resources

CloudFormation will only update a custom resource if its parameters change, not if the underlying Lambda function changes. This is normally OK, but not in our case. We want to execute the custom resource automatically if any files in the web-site directory change, and CloudFormation thinks that those files are the source code for the Lambda function.

To trick CloudFormation into running the SiteSource function whenever its files change, we need to add a property to the custom resource that will be different with each function update. That's why the SiteSource function from the previous listing automatically publishes a Lambda alias (line 148), and why the DeploymentResource contains a Version parameter pointing to the published Lambda version (line 159). This parameter is not strictly required by the DeployToS3 application, but using a numerically incrementing version ensures that the web files are always consistent with our API.

Notice that SiteSource.Version in line 159 is a reference, not an attribute, so we use !Ref to read it. This is a curiosity of SAM version publishing. When you use the AutoPublishAlias property of a function resource, SAM automatically stores the resulting version in a new reference, which it names by appending .Version to the function name.

Build, package and deploy the application again. Remember to add CAPABILITY_AUTO_EXPAND when deploying, so CloudFormation can process nested applications. Once the application is deployed, get the stack outputs to discover the website endpoint URL, and open it in your browser. Check out the source code of the page, and you should see that the placeholder in the index page was replaced with the full URL of the actual API (Figure 11.2).

```
1  <html>
2    <body>
3      <div step="initial">
4        <h1>Select a file</h1>
5        <input type="hidden" id="apiurl" value="https://6mb2087x87.execute-api.us-east-1.amazonaws.com/api/" />
6        <input type="file" id="picker"/>
7      </div>
8      <div step="uploading" style="display: none">
9        Please wait, uploading...
10       <br/>
11       <progress id="progressbar" max="100" value="0" />
12     </div>
13     <div step="converting" style="display: none">
14       Please wait, converting your file...
15     </div>
16     <div step="result" style="display: none">
17       <h1>Your thumbnail is ready</h1>
18       <a id="resultlink">download it</a>
19     </div>
20     <div step="error" style="display: none">
21       <h1>There was an error creating the thumbnail</h1>
22       <p id="errortext"></p>
23     </div>
24     <script src="user-workflow.js"></script>
25   </body>
26 </html>
```

Figure 11.2: *DeployToS3 replaces the placeholder with the actual API URL during deployment.*

Try uploading a JPG file using the new web page. You should see a progress bar while the browser is transferring your file (Figure 11.3). The client code will also wait until the result is ready to show the download link, making the user experience a lot less error prone.

Figure 11.3: *Moving session workflow out of Lambda functions to the client allows us to reduce costs but also create a nicer experience, such as by displaying progress bars.*

Uploading files without the SAR component

The DeployToS3 AWS Serverless Application repository component can handle basic upload tasks easily. For more complex scenarios, such as individually controlling caching or response headers for files, you can use the AWS command line tools and somehow coordinate CloudFormation template deployment with uploading web assets.

The aws s3 tool has a convenient option for synchronising a local directory with an S3 bucket. Here is the basic form for how to use it:

```
aws s3 sync <LOCAL DIR> s3://<BUCKET>/<PREFIX>
```

To make files publicly accessible, add --acl public-read. The command has many more options, such as for adding or removing groups of files, and setting caching headers and similar properties. Check out the S3 sync[8] documentation page for more information.

AWS also has a workflow product for deploying front-end applications, called AWS Amplify Console[9]. It might be worth investigating if you want to build and deploy complex front ends to serverless applications.

---

[8]https://docs.aws.amazon.com/cli/latest/reference/s3/sync.html
[9]https://aws.amazon.com/amplify/console/

We now have a nice baseline for an application. In the next chapter, we'll make the API more robust and deal with other tasks, such as testing, required before our application is truly ready to accept real users.

Interesting experiments

- Make the client web page page attractive by styling it using CSS.
- Configure a CloudFront CDN to compress and locally cache static assets, and reconfigure the application so users access it through the CDN.
- The error handling in this chapter only acts on problems during file upload, not on problems during file conversion. Using the dead-letter queue technique from Chapter 9, detect conversion errors and save a marker error file somewhere on S3 where the client can detect it. Then change the client-side workflow to poll for that file while waiting on results and notify clients about conversion errors.

12. Designing robust applications

This chapter explains how to structure SAM application templates and source code to make it easy to support, maintain and evolve applications in the future. You will also learn about protecting serverless applications against abuse.

To avoid conflicts between user uploads, the ShowFormFunction function we created in Chapter 10 creates a random upload key and appends the .jpg image extension. In the previous chapter, we made user interactions much nicer, but we're still restricting users to converting JPG images. ImageMagick can handle many image formats easily, so we can make the application a lot more useful by letting users upload PNG and GIF images as well.

To support multiple formats, we just need to ensure that users upload images to S3 with the correct extensions, so ImageMagick can load the files appropriately. Restricting uploads to .jpg was necessary in Chapter 10, because we had no client-facing logic. ShowFormFunction needs to limit the uploads to something, and the client couldn't specify up front what it wants. Now that the client code is smarter, it could ask for an upload policy for a specific image type.

API endpoints with path parameters

So far in this book, we have built API endpoints with parameters either in the query string or the request body. There is one more option: we could put parameters in the request paths. For example, requests to /sign/jpg could produce policies for a jpg file upload, and requests to /sign/png could do the same for png files.

We could create individual endpoints for each file type, but this would complicate the application template unnecessarily. Extending the application to support more file types would require changing the template and the application code, and it would be error prone. API Gateway has a much simpler solution for cases when a part of the request path needs to be flexible. Declare an API endpoint using a parameter name in curly braces, and API Gateway will use it for all matching requests. For example, we can create a single endpoint using the path /sign/{extension}, and it will handle requests for /sign/png, /sign/jpg, /sign/gif and any other request starting with /sign/ in the future. To read out the value of a parameter from the path in a Lambda function, we can use the pathParameters field of the API Gateway event.

Any component of a path can contain a parameter, so endpoints such as /sign/{extension}/image are also OK. You can also add multiple generic components to the same endpoint, for example /sign/{extension}/image/{size}. The parameters are not completely arbitrary, though. API Gateway matches paths on non-parameterised parts and requires all endpoint paths to be unique, so we can't create /sign/{extension} and /sign/{type} at the same time; API Gateway would not know how to choose between them. We'd have to add something extra to those paths to make them distinguishable. Also, only full path components can be parameters. API Gateway treats a forward slash (/) as a component separator. While /sign/{extension}/image and /sign/{extension}/type would be perfectly valid paths, /sign/image.{extension} and /sign/{extension}-type would not.

API Gateway does not validate path parameters, so it's not possible to set constraints directly in the API definition. For example, /sign/{extension} will match requests to /sign/png, but also to /sign/xls. Although ImageMagick supports lots of image types, it's still not magic enough to generate thumbnails for Excel files.

Greedy path parameters

In addition to individual path components, you can also use a *greedy parameter*, which matches one or more path components. Just include a plus sign at the end of the component name, for example /sign/{proxy+}. This will match /sign/jpg and /sign/jpg/size/500. This is a useful trick if you want to build your own request routing inside a Lambda function.

To prevent user errors, we will need to validate extensions using a list of supported types in the Lambda function connected to the API endpoint.

Let's add another parameter to our application template, so we can configure the supported file types easily. Add the block from the following listing to the Parameters section of your application template, indented to align with other parameters (for example ThumbnailWidth).

―――――――――――― ch12/template.yaml ――――――――――――

```
AllowedImageExtensions:
  Type: String
  Default: jpg,jpeg,png,gif
  Description: Comma-delimited list of allowed image file extensions (lowercase)
```

We can now change the ShowFormFunction function configuration. We'll need to update the request path to include a generic path parameter (line 88 in the following listing), and add another environment variable to pass allowed types (line 97). The rest of the function configuration stays the same.

―――――――――――― ch12/template.yaml ――――――――――――

```
ShowFormFunction:
  Type: AWS::Serverless::Function
  Properties:
    CodeUri: user-form/
    Handler: show-form.lambdaHandler
    Runtime: nodejs12.x
    Events:
      ShowForm:
        Type: Api
        Properties:
          Path: /sign/{extension}
          Method: get
          RestApiId: !Ref WebApi
    Environment:
      Variables:
        UPLOAD_S3_BUCKET: !Ref UploadS3Bucket
        UPLOAD_LIMIT_IN_MB: !Ref UploadLimitInMb
        CORS_ORIGIN: !GetAtt WebAssetsS3Bucket.WebsiteURL
```

```
96            THUMBNAILS_S3_BUCKET: !Ref ThumbnailsS3Bucket
97            ALLOWED_IMAGE_EXTENSIONS: !Ref AllowedImageExtensions
98        Policies:
99          - S3FullAccessPolicy:
100             BucketName: !Ref UploadS3Bucket
101          - S3ReadPolicy:
102             BucketName: !Ref ThumbnailsS3Bucket
```

On the client side, we'll need to modify the getSignatures function to add the file extension to the API call. Let's use this opportunity to make the function a bit more robust as well, and check whether the API responded with an HTTP OK (200) or not. Any application with remote network components might experience occasional transport errors. WiFi networks might drop, or users might move from one mobile network cell to another or be working on a very slow connection. Likewise, the back end might not be available to respond to user requests. AWS infrastructure is highly scalable and available, but nobody in the world is guaranteeing 100% uptime. (AWS Service Level Agreement[1] for API Gateway is 99.95%.) We should verify the network response and show a useful error message in the event of trouble. Change the function in user-workflow.js to match the following lines.

─────────────── ch12/web-site/user-workflow.js ───────────────

```
1   async function getSignatures(apiUrl, extension) {
2     if (!apiUrl) {
3       throw 'Please provide an API URL';
4     }
5     if (!extension) {
6       throw 'Please provide an extension';
7     }
8     const response = await fetch(`${apiUrl}sign/${extension}`);
9     if (response.ok) {
10      return response.json();
11    } else {
12      const error = await response.text();
13      throw error;
14    }
15  };
```

We'll also need to change the main workflow function to get the extension of the proposed file upload and pass it on to getSignatures. Change the startUpload function to match the following listing (the relevant changes are in lines 126-131).

─────────────── ch12/web-site/user-workflow.js ───────────────

```
118  async function startUpload(evt) {
119    const picker = evt.target;
120    const file = picker.files && picker.files[0];
```

---

[1]https://aws.amazon.com/api-gateway/sla/

```
const apiUrl = document.getElementById('apiurl').value;

if (file && file.name) {
  picker.value = '';
  try {
    const extension = file.name.replace(/.+\./g, '');
    if (!extension) {
      throw `${file.name} has no extension`;
    }
    showStep('uploading');
    const signatures = await getSignatures(apiUrl, extension);
    console.log('got signatures', signatures);
    await uploadBlob(signatures.upload, file, progressNotifier);
    showStep('converting');
    await pollForResult(signatures.download, 3000, 20);
    const downloadLink = document.getElementById('resultlink');
    downloadLink.setAttribute('href', signatures.download);
    showStep('result');
  } catch (e) {
    console.error(e);
    const displayError = e.message || JSON.stringify(e);
    document.getElementById('errortext').innerHTML = displayError;
    showStep('error');
  }
}
};
```

Designing with Ports and Adapters

Next, we'll need to modify the ShowFormFunction Lambda function to validate the requested extension and return an error message in case of unsupported extensions. The function we wrote in the previous chapter was still relatively easy to read and understand. Putting more logic into that function definitely pushes it beyond the threshold of what I'd consider simple.

A big part of making robust code is the ability to understand it easily and modify it with confidence. Both those goals can be greatly helped by some nice unit tests. However, our current function design is not really making that easy. The function directly talks to S3, requiring IAM privileges to execute, and it depends on several environment variables that need to be configured up front. Automated tests for this function would be slow and error prone, and it would be difficult to set up all the testing dependencies. This would be a good time to redesign the code and prepare it for future evolution.

At MindMup, we use the *Ports and Adapters*[2] design pattern (also called *hexagonal architecture*) for any but the simplest Lambda functions. This makes it easy to cover the code with automated tests at various levels effectively, and evolve functions easily over time. The pattern was first described by Alistair Cockburn in 2005. It's very closely related to the idea of *Simplicators*, presented by Nat Pryce and Steve Freeman in *Growing Object-Oriented Software*[3], and the idea of *anti-corruption layers*, described by Eric Evans in *Domain-Driven Design*[4].

The purpose of this design pattern, straight from its canonical description, is to 'allow an application to equally be driven by users, programs, automated test or batch scripts, and to be developed and tested in isolation from its eventual runtime devices and databases'. Cockburn observed that when business logic gets entangled with external interactions, both become difficult to develop and test. This applies equally to user interface interactions (such as receiving requests from web pages) and to infrastructure interactions (for example saving to a database or acting on queue messages). Lambda code might not have any direct user interactions, but it is always triggered by infrastructure events and often needs to talk to other infrastructure, so this makes Lambda functions prone to the problems that Ports and Adapters addresses.

The design pattern suggests isolating the business logic into a core that has no external interactions but instead provides various interfaces for interactions (Figure 12.1). These interfaces are the *ports*, and they are described in the domain model of the business logic. For each type of interaction, we implement the relevant port interface with an *adapter*, which translates from the core model into the specific infrastructure API. Test versions of adapters can help us experiment with the business logic in the core easily, in memory, without any specific setup or access to test infrastructure. This means that we could run a huge number of automated tests for the business logic core quickly and reliably. A much smaller number of integration tests, focused around adapters, can prove the necessary subset of interactions with real infrastructure. Designing with ports and adapters also allows the easy swapping of one infrastructure for another if they serve the same purpose, for example moving external storage from S3 to DynamoDB.

To apply this pattern to Lambda functions, we usually split the code into three parts:

1. The request processor, representing the core business logic
2. Concrete adapters for interaction ports, usually one for each type of infrastructure
3. The Lambda entry point, responsible for wiring everything together

The first component, the request processor, is responsible for encapsulating the business logic. It does not talk directly to any AWS resources such as S3. It does not care about the Lambda interfaces such as environment variables or context objects. It does not worry about returning values or reporting errors in a way that Lambda can understand. Ideally, it does not load any third-party libraries. We configure the request processor by passing specific adapters into the constructor method. Apart from the constructor, the request processor usually has only one other method, which starts the request execution. This method should use names, relationships and concepts described in the language of the business domain, including parameters, return values, exceptions and internal processing. The interactions between this method and abstract ports effectively define the collaborator interfaces. We usually cover this with extensive unit tests, using test doubles or mocks as adapters for ports.

---

[2]http://wiki.c2.com/?PortsAndAdaptersArchitecture
[3]https://amzn.to/2TAqYmJ
[4]https://amzn.to/2ER9mIR

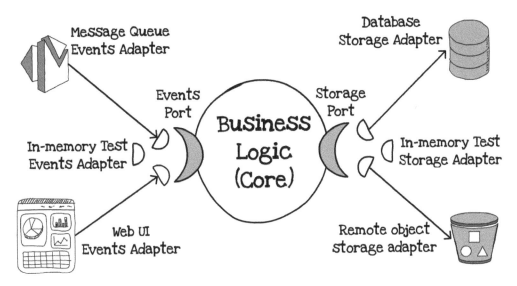

Figure 12.1: *Ports and Adapters design pattern separates business logic from infrastructure and interfaces. Individual adapters implement port interfaces to interact with the core, and can be easily replaced with other adapter implementations.*

Each infrastructure port gets implemented by a concrete adapter that can load the AWS SDK or any other third-party libraries. Individual adapters are typically separate classes. These classes must not assume they are running in Lambda, so they can't access environment variables or the Lambda context. For any such dependencies, these classes provide constructor arguments. We usually do not write unit tests for those, but cover them with integration tests that talk to a real infrastructure component. For example, tests would create an S3 bucket, try out the adapter methods, and then remove the bucket at the end.

The Lambda entry-point code is responsible for setting up the application components and translating between the business logic core and the Lambda environment. This is where we consume environment variables and the Lambda context, translate between the Lambda event and the parameters of the request processor, and format results or errors in a way that the Lambda infrastructure expects. If this becomes complicated, we may extract bits into utility functions. Utility functions usually get covered with unit tests. The main Lambda function is usually trivially simple, so it does not get covered by unit tests. If it's not possible to make it trivially simple, it will gets covered by smoke tests that can run after deployment.

Request processor

For the ShowFormFunction handler, the core business logic is to validate that a requested upload has an extension, and that the extension belongs to a list of approved file types. For valid extensions, the function needs to create a unique upload file name based on the request ID and the extension, and produce a signed upload policy and a signed download policy. This business core will have three ports (Figure 12.2):

1. The first port should provide the request ID and the extension, starting the process, and format the resulting signatures accordingly.

2. The second port should sign upload policies based on a key.
3. The third port should sign download policies based on a key.

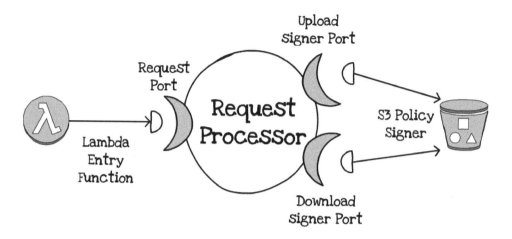

Figure 12.2: *Ports and adapters for signing S3 policies using Lambda functions*

The core business logic should not care about AWS interfaces, but instead describe the workflow using concepts important for a specific use case, such as signing uploads and downloads. Create a new file called request-processor.js in the user-form directory with the code from the following listing.

—————————————— ch12/user-form/request-processor.js ——————————————

```
 1  module.exports = class RequestProcessor {
 2    constructor(uploadSigner, downloadSigner, uploadLimitInMB, allowedExtensions) {
 3      this.uploadSigner = uploadSigner;
 4      this.downloadSigner = downloadSigner;
 5      this.uploadLimitInMB = uploadLimitInMB;
 6      this.allowedExtensions = allowedExtensions;
 7    };
 8    processRequest(requestId, extension) {
 9      if (!extension) {
10        throw `no extension provided`;
11      }
12      const normalisedExtension = extension.toLowerCase();
13      const isImage = this.allowedExtensions.includes(normalisedExtension);
14      if (!isImage) {
15        throw `extension ${extension} is not supported`;
16      }
17      const fileKey = `${requestId}.${normalisedExtension}`;
18      return {
```

```
49    upload: this.uploadSigner.signUpload(fileKey, this.uploadLimitInMB),
20    download: this.downloadSigner.signDownload(fileKey)
21    };
22  };
23 };
```

Writing unit tests for core components

We can test the RequestProcessor class in isolation, without network access or talking to actual AWS services. During the test setup, we could create simple in-memory adapters for the ports required by the workflow. The next listing shows how what a unit test would look like using jest, a popular JavaScript unit testing tool.

———————————————— ch12/user-form/tests/request-processor.test.js ————————————————

```
1   const RequestProcessor = require('../request-processor');
2   describe('request-processor', () => {
3     let uploadSigner, downloadSigner,
4       uploadLimit, allowedExtensions, underTest;
5     beforeEach(() => {
6       uploadSigner = {
7         signUpload: jest.fn((key, limit) => `upload-max-${limit}-${key}`)
8       };
9       downloadSigner = {
10        signDownload: jest.fn((key) => `download-${key}`)
11      };
12      uploadLimit = 10;
13      allowedExtensions = 'jpg,gif';
14      underTest = new RequestProcessor(
15        uploadSigner, downloadSigner, uploadLimit, allowedExtensions
16      );
17    });
18    describe('processRequest', () => {
19      test('rejects request without an extension', () => {
20        expect(() => underTest.processRequest('req-id'))
21          .toThrow('no extension provided');
22      });
23      test('rejects requests with an unsupported extension', () => {
24        expect(() => underTest.processRequest('req-id', 'xls'))
25          .toThrow('extension xls is not supported');
26      });
27      test('signs a request for supported extensions', () => {
28        expect(underTest.processRequest('req-id', 'jpg'))
29          .toEqual({
30            "download": "download-req-id.jpg",
```

```
31          "upload": "upload-max-10-req-id.jpg"
32        });
33      });
34    });
35  });
```

Of course, this is just a start. To keep things simple in this book, I've listed only the basic test cases. In a real project, I would add examples for important edge cases.

Isolating the business logic core from infrastructure allows us to quickly check various boundary conditions, and providing simple in-memory implementations for port interfaces lets us reason about the system under test easily. We don't have to worry about the complexity of the SIGV4 process, differences between AWS endpoints in various regions, and network communications. All that can be tested separately, with an integration test for actual infrastructure adapters.

Excluding test resources from deployment

Once we start putting tests and testing tools into the project, we need to reconfigure Lambda packaging. There's no reason to include test cases, libraries and tools (such as jest) in the deployment package SAM sends to Lambda. SAM can help create a minimal clean package during the sam build step, but it is not smart enough to guess all the possible testing tools. It does, however, understand project manifests for many popular programming languages, so it's really important to properly specify the type of testing dependencies.

For JavaScript, that means using the devDependencies section of package.json (or installing NPM packages using the -D flag) for third-party tools you want to exclude from Lambda packaging. In the case of Node.js functions, SAM also uses the standard npm pack configuration to decide whether to include source files in a package. This means that you can explicitly list required files in the files section of package.json, or exclude directories and files by adding them to a file called .npmignore in the project directory. For example, the package manifest from the following listing would ensure that only root-level javascript files are included (so excluding the tests subdirectory) and that jest is available for development but never uploaded to Lambda.

———————————————— ch12/user-form/tests/package.json ————————————————

```
1  {
2    "name": "user-form",
3    "version": "1.0.0",
4    "license": "MIT",
5    "files": [
6      "*.js"
7    ],
8    "scripts": {
9      "test": "jest"
10   },
11   "devDependencies": {
```

```
    "got": "^9.6.0",
    "jest": "^24.8.0"
  }
}
```

Infrastructure adapters

We need a concrete implementation of the upload and download signer ports which can talk to AWS S3. These two operations are closely related, so we can put them both in the same class. This class is specific for S3, so it can use the AWS SDK classes. Create a file called s3-policy-signer.js in the user-form Lambda directory, with the code from the following listing.

———————————————————— ch12/user-form/s3-policy-signer.js ————————————————————

```
1  const aws = require('aws-sdk');
2  const s3 = new aws.S3();
3  module.exports = class S3PolicySigner {
4    constructor(bucketName, expiry) {
5      this.bucketName = bucketName;
6      this.expiry = expiry || 600;
7    };
8    signUpload(key, uploadLimitInMB) {
9      const uploadParams = {
10       Bucket: this.bucketName,
11       Expires: this.expiry,
12       Conditions: [
13         ['content-length-range', 1, uploadLimitInMB * 1000000]
14       ],
15       Fields: { acl: 'private', key: key }
16     };
17     return s3.createPresignedPost(uploadParams);
18   };
19   signDownload(key) {
20     const downloadParams = {
21       Bucket: this.bucketName,
22       Key: key,
23       Expires: this.expiry
24     };
25     return s3.getSignedUrl('getObject', downloadParams);
26   };
27 };
```

Similar to the request processor test, we could set up a small integration test for this class that uploads a file to S3, generates a signature, and tries to download it just to make sure that the whole process works end to end. The following listing shows what such a test would look like using jest.

———————————————————— ch12/user-form/tests/s3-policy-signer.test.js ——————————

```
const aws = require('aws-sdk'),
  get = require('got'),
  s3 = new aws.S3(),
  S3PolicySigner = require('../s3-policy-signer');
describe('s3-policy-signer', () => {
  let bucketName;
  beforeAll(() => {
    jest.setTimeout(10000);
    bucketName = `test-signer-${Date.now()}`;
    return s3.createBucket({Bucket: bucketName}).promise();
  });
  afterAll(() => {
    return s3.deleteBucket({Bucket: bucketName}).promise();
  });
  describe('signDownload', () => {
    let fileKey;
    beforeEach(() => {
      fileKey = `test-file-${Date.now()}`;
      return s3.putObject({
        Bucket: bucketName,
        Key: fileKey,
        Body: 'test-file-contents'
      }).promise();
    });
    afterEach(() => {
      return s3.deleteObject({
        Bucket: bucketName, Key: fileKey
      }).promise();
    });
    test('produces a URL allowing direct HTTPS access', () => {
      const underTest = new S3PolicySigner(bucketName, 600);
      const url = underTest.signDownload(fileKey);
      return get(url)
        .then(r => expect(r.body).toEqual('test-file-contents'));
    });
  });
});
```

This test will run several orders of magnitude more slowly than the request processor unit test, because it uses network infrastructure and creates and removes files and buckets. We could in theory provide a test stub class for the AWS SDK to speed things up, but we would lose a lot of the confidence. Using a stub would only prove that our adapter calls the SDK as expected, not that the whole process works. For integration tests, I prefer to test the actual infrastructure.

The Ports and Adapters pattern enabled us to separate business logic code from integration code, so we can also separate business logic tests from integration tests. We can run lots of different checks and evaluate expectations for business logic code quickly, without access to any network infrastructure, then run a few slow infrastructural tests independently from that.

If you want to avoid using the actual AWS stack in your tests, and prefer to have a local simulation, check out the LocalStack[5] project.

Lambda utility methods

We have already used json-response.js to format JSON objects into something that Lambda can understand, but this method loaded the CORS origin from the process environment, which should be the responsibility of the Lambda entry point. Remove the process variable and add it as another regular argument, so we can easily test this method.

──────────────── ch12/user-form/json-response.js ────────────────

```
1  module.exports = function jsonResponse(body, corsOrigin) {
2    return {
3      statusCode: 200,
4      body: JSON.stringify(body),
5      headers: {
6        'Content-Type': 'application/json',
7        'Access-Control-Allow-Origin': corsOrigin
8      }
9    };
10 };
```

When only the Lambda entry point depends on the actual Lambda infrastructure, we can cover utility methods with focused in-memory tests. The next listing shows what a test for the jsonResponse function would look like using jest (again, for simplicity, I've only included the basic test cases, but in a real project I would include many more boundary scenarios).

──────────────── ch12/user-form/tests/json-response.test.js ────────────────

```
1  const jsonResponse = require('../json-response');
2  describe('jsonResponse', () => {
3    it('responds with HTTP code 200', () => {
4      const result = jsonResponse('body', 'origin');
5      expect(result.statusCode).toEqual(200);
6    });
7    it('includes the CORS origin', () => {
8      const result = jsonResponse('body', 'https://gojko.net');
9      expect(result.headers['Access-Control-Allow-Origin'])
10       .toEqual('https://gojko.net');
```

───────────────────

[5]https://github.com/localstack/localstack

```
11    });
12    it('formats objects as JSON strings', () => {
13      const result = jsonResponse({a: 11, b: {c: 1}});
14      expect(result.body).toEqual('{"a":11,"b":{"c":1}}');
15    });
16    it('uses the JSON content type', () => {
17      const result = jsonResponse('body', 'origin');
18      expect(result.headers['Content-Type'])
19        .toEqual('application/json');
20    });
21  });
```

We'll need another utility method to report errors back. JavaScript is specific regarding error handling, because it can pass around exceptions or strings or just plain objects as errors, so we need to ensure that all the options are converted into a string. We'll also pass a generic HTTP error code 500 back, instead of the 200 which signals success. Create a file called error-response.js in the user-form Lambda directory, with the following code.

—————————————— ch12/user-form/error-response.js ——————————————

```
1   module.exports = function errorResponse(body, corsOrigin) {
2     return {
3       statusCode: 500,
4       body: String(body),
5       headers: {
6         'Content-Type': 'text/plain',
7         'Access-Control-Allow-Origin': corsOrigin
8       }
9     };
10  };
```

The test cases for errorResponse would look be similar to the tests for jsonResponse, so I will omit them from this book. You can write them for homework.

Lambda entry code

The main Lambda file now just needs to connect all the dots. It should load the configuration from environment variables, parse events and variables correctly, and format the results and errors. Change the show-form.js file to match the following listing.

—————————————— ch12/user-form/show-form.js ——————————————

```
1   const jsonResponse = require('./json-response');
2   const errorResponse = require('./error-response');
3   const RequestProcessor = require('./request-processor');
```

```
const S3PolicySigner = require('./s3-policy-signer');
exports.lambdaHandler = async (event, context) => {
  try {
    const uploadSigner = new S3PolicySigner(process.env.UPLOAD_S3_BUCKET);
    const downloadSigner = new S3PolicySigner(process.env.THUMBNAILS_S3_BUCKET);
    const requestProcessor = new RequestProcessor(
      uploadSigner,
      downloadSigner,
      parseInt(process.env.UPLOAD_LIMIT_IN_MB),
      process.env.ALLOWED_IMAGE_EXTENSIONS.split(',')
    );
    const result = requestProcessor.processRequest(
      context.awsRequestId,
      event.pathParameters.extension,
    );
    return jsonResponse(result, process.env.CORS_ORIGIN);
  } catch (e) {
    return errorResponse(e, process.env.CORS_ORIGIN);
  }
};
```

At MindMup, we usually do not write automated tests for Lambda entry points. Instead, we manually validate them during exploratory testing. The major risk for such code is bad configuration, and automated tests before deployment do not address that risk at all. A quick manual check after deployment can easily prove that everything is connected correctly. For more complex scenarios, you can add automated smoke tests that prove that the function connects adapters and request processors correctly, and include them into a gradual deployment process as explained in Chapter 5.

Rebuild, package and deploy the template now. Then open the web app page and try loading a PDF file. You should see an error message telling you that the app cannot create PDF templates yet (Figure 12.3).

Protecting against abuse

So far, we have worked on making the application more robust by making it more generic and providing better error reporting.

Another important aspect of robustness is to mitigate the negative effects of abuse. Our API is currently completely exposed to the internet. A billion people coming to the app could start a billion requests, and AWS will happily scale things up to serve that. Magically autoscaling architectures that charge for usage are great when you need to satisfy increasing demand, but they can also be a financial risk. One of the biggest concerns people have when migrating to serverless applications is how to protect against someone starting a billion requests just to try to bring our system down or to cause financial damage by racking up our AWS bill. The level of this exposure, of course, depends on your risk profile, so it's difficult to provide a generic solution to this problem. However, here are some ideas that might make it easier to manage that situation.

Figure 12.3: *Our application flow can now show an error message if users try to upload an unsupported file, instead of the application just timing out.*

API throttling

API Gateway can automatically throttle requests before even passing them on to the back-end integration, so one easy way of controlling the risk of abuse is to limit the number of requests coming through the API. You can configure throttling for burst requests per second or steady-state requests per second, by using the MethodSettings property of of the API resource with SAM. You can set this in the Globals section for implicitly defined APIs, or in the properties of an individual AWS::Serverless::Api resource. For example, we can set up throttling for all the endpoints in our API by using the configuration from the following listing (the new lines are 73-77).

──────────────────────── ch12/template.yaml ────────────────────────

```
68   WebApi:
69     Type: AWS::Serverless::Api
70     Properties:
71       StageName: !Ref AppStage
72       Cors: !Sub "'${WebAssetsS3Bucket.WebsiteURL}'"
73       MethodSettings:
74         - ResourcePath: '/*'
75           HttpMethod: '*'
76           ThrottlingBurstLimit: 20
77           ThrottlingRateLimit: 10
```

If the number of requests exceeds the limit, API Gateway will start responding with 429 Too Many Requests.

Our client application code is now more robust, so it will show the error to the client, but we could potentially change it to pause a bit and then retry automatically. For more information on API Gateway throttling, check out the page *Throttle API Requests for Better Throughput*[6] in the API Gateway documentation.

SAM allows you to set global limits for an API stage easily, but not for individual users. API Gateway actually supports different throttling limits for different users, authenticated using API keys. You can create individual usage plans and, for example, apply a different API key for authenticated users and anonymous requests, or provide individual enterprise users with their own API keys. You then need to configure the API to require a key for invocation. For information about that, see the *Controlling Access to API Gateway APIs*[7] page from the SAM Developer Guide.

Lambda throttling

API throttling can only protect functions invoked through API Gateway. We also have a function triggered automatically once a file is uploaded to S3, without an API in front of it. We can limit financial risk from such Lambda functions in two ways.

The first is to restrict the time allowed for execution. If someone keeps uploading massive files that require long conversions, we could tell Lambda to just interrupt those processes instead of letting them run to the end. For that, use the Timeout setting on the individual function. You'll need to balance this with giving the function enough time to complete the expected tasks. We're currently setting this to 600, which is 10 minutes.

The second method to limit financial risk from Lambda functions is to control the number of concurrent executions for the function. This is effectively throttling requests on the Lambda level. By default, AWS limits concurrent executions to 1000 Lambda instances for a single AWS account (you can increase this limit by contacting AWS support). Individual Lambda functions can request a much lower limit by using the ReservedConcurrentExecutions property. This is a good way to limit exposure for risky functions. For example, let's allow only up to 10 instances of the conversion function to run at any given time. Add the code from the following listing to the Properties section of the ConvertFileFunction resource (indented so it is aligned with other properties, for example MemorySize).

─────────────────── ch12/template.yaml ───────────────────

```
123   ReservedConcurrentExecutions: 10
```

For more information on concurrency controls for Lambda functions, check out the page *Managing Concurrency*[8] in AWS Lambda documentation.

---

[6]https://docs.aws.amazon.com/apigateway/latest/developerguide/api-gateway-request-throttling.html
[7]https://docs.aws.amazon.com/serverless-application-model/latest/developerguide/serverless-controlling-access-to-apis.html
[8]https://docs.aws.amazon.com/lambda/latest/dg/concurrent-executions.html

Monitoring throttling

We can use CloudWatch alerts to notify us about throttling events, in a similar way to how we used it to monitor for errors in the section *Adding deployment alerts* in Chapter 5. CloudWatch automatically tracks Lambda throttles with the Throttles metric inside the AWS/Lambda namespace. There's no specific throttling metric for API Gateway, but a slightly wider metric monitors all errors with codes between 400 and 499. Add an alert for the 4XXError metric inside the AWS/ApiGateway namespace to learn about it.

We now have an application that is ready to receive millions of users and produce thumbnails for a variety of image formats. It does not cost anything when people are not using it, and scales automatically depending on the actual workload. Most of the operational tasks are handled by AWS, included in the price of Lambda calls. Our code is nicely structured, covered by some basic automated tests, so it will be very easy to maintain and extend in the future. You can use this code as a template for a huge number of use cases when users submit tasks and your application needs to handle them asynchronously.

In the final chapter of this book, we'll investigate how to design and structure more complex applications.

Interesting experiments

- If you added a Lambda layer for FFMpeg as suggested in the experiments at the end of Chapter 10, then modify the request processor to allow the uploading of videos, and introduce another port and adapter for video thumbnails.
- Configure throttling to allow only one or two concurrent executions, and then try uploading many images in quick succession. Check CloudWatch logs and metrics to spot the throttling in action.
- Change the client workflow code to check for throttled requests, and handle them by pausing and retrying automatically.
- Add a few more test cases to improve test coverage. For example, add a test case for generating the upload policy.

13. Deployment options

In the final chapter of this book, you'll learn about common ways of structuring applications with Lambda functions.

Serverless architectures are still a relatively novel way of deploying applications, and it's too early to talk about generally applicable design patterns or best practices. The community is still discovering how best to use this type of deployment architecture, and the platform is still frequently changing. There are, however, some good design practices worth considering when you are thinking about structuring applications with Lambda functions. As closing remarks for the book, I'd like to offer some ideas that helped us build and maintain MindMup efficiently. Hopefully they will help you start thinking about organising your applications around Lambda functions in an effective way.

Think about jobs, not functions

AWS Lambda quietly appeared on the scene in 2014, several years before 'serverless' became a buzzword. Back then, the DevOps community was trying to figure out the right relationship between applications, virtual machines and containers. Tool vendors were competing on how many times they could cram 'microservices' into their ads. 'Monolith' became a dirty word. AWS product managers decided to introduce a new term, and called their deployment units 'functions'. My best guess is that they did it on purpose to signal a generational shift in deployment architecture. To avoid comparisons with older products, they chose a name that did not come with a lot of existing connotations, at least not in the deployment area. However, the name Lambda has a very specific meaning in functional programming, which itself is based on a branch of mathematics called *Lambda calculus*. Mention Lambdas and functions together, and people with any experience of functional programming immediately make wrong assumptions about the AWS Lambda platform, such as that it is stateless, or that it can parallelise calculations automatically. That's why we need to unpick a terminological mess in order to discuss design and architecture of applications based on cloud functions.

People influenced by the functional programming terminology often think that a Lambda function needs to be a small isolated piece of code with a single purpose (single processing function), and that it is stateless (or, in the functional terminology, that is has no side-effects). None of those assumptions are true.

I've mostly used very simple functions as examples in this book, not because Lambda functions have to be simple, but because complex code isn't good for teaching. A single Lambda function can have a deployment package up to 250 MB, more than enough for an enterprise application server along with all the entity and session beans a UML architect can draw in a lifetime. There's nothing preventing you from bundling a big monolithic website and deploying it as a single Lambda function. Likewise, there's nothing preventing you from deploying an API where each individual endpoint is handled by a separate Lambda function, served by hundreds of other Lambda functions that perform background tasks. And, of course, anything between those two extremes is also possible.

AWS Lambda function invocations are not technically independent, and assuming that they are can cause subtle problems. Lambda will often reuse existing container instances over a short period of time, to speed up processing and avoid cold starts. The initialisation code for the functions runs only once on start, not for each request, and the process in a Lambda instance keeps running to handle subsequent requests. For

JavaScript, this means that any variables or modules you load outside the Lambda event handler stay around between two different requests. Leaving a mess in internal memory state during one request can unexpectedly hurt when the next request comes in.

Lambda containers also have a temporary disk space (512 MB[1] available under /tmp), and two different requests executing on the same function instance can in theory share data by reading and writing files there. If your code writes to the temporary disk space and does not clean up after each request, the function instance will at some point run out of available space.

On the other hand, the fact that a Lambda function can have side-effects opens up some very nice opportunities. For example, the total size for a Lambda function package needs to be under 250 MB, including all layers. One way to work around that limit is to put the additional code on S3, compressed into an archive, instead of a Lambda layer. The Lambda function can then be just a small skeleton initialiser which downloads and unpacks the additional resources from S3 to the temporary disk space when it starts. Because the temporary space is shared between function executions, this costly initialisation can happen only once per cold start, and most requests will not suffer from the additional overhead.

People influenced by the container and DevOps terminology often think about Lambda functions as services, but that comparison also has problems. Traditional container-based services are usually stateful and long-running, with the application developers controlling routing. Lambda fully controls routing, starting and shutting down containers, and application developers don't have any control over it. Lambda functions aren't really stateless or stateful, they are transient.

Another common misconception about Lambda deployments is that it's impossible to control data ownership across instances. Lambda is an auto-scaling platform, but this doesn't mean that it has to scale. As an extreme example, it's quite easy create a proper monolith. In Chapter 12, I showed you how to control function concurrency limits in order to prevent abuse from runaway functions and denial-of-service attacks. By setting the concurrency limit of a function to 1, you can ensure that AWS never runs more than one instance of that code in parallel. Lambda will create the function container when it's needed, and shut it down when there's no more demand. For an occasional task, using single-instance Lambda functions might be cheaper and easier to manage than similar code running within an AWS Elastic Compute Cloud (EC2) container. For a sustained load over a longer period of time, this would be several times more expensive than an EC2 machine, but, given that it's a single instance, would not really break the bank.

Instead of thinking about deploying functions or services, I find it more useful to think about structuring Lambda functions around discrete jobs which don't necessarily perform a single code function. Instead of thinking about stateless or stateful services, it's more useful to design for share-nothing architecture, when different parts can own data and share state, but different functions and instances of a single function don't actively share data between themselves.

One Lambda or many?

The common wisdom today seems to be that monolithic code is bad and that micro-services are good, but I disagree. Monoliths are usually simpler to develop and manage than a network of services, and in many

---

[1]https://docs.aws.amazon.com/lambda/latest/dg/limits.html

cases significantly faster to deploy. Dividing code and data into multiple machines always introduces a huge amount of complexity related to synchronisation and consistency, which simply does not exist when everything is in a single memory space. Lambda provides many options for breaking down or aggregating processing, and it's important to look at the platform constraints so you can decide which is the best solution in a particular case.

Aggregate processing data ownership

The first important constraint of the Lambda platform is that application developers do not control request routing. Two logically related requests, for example coming from the same user or related to the same data entity, might be received by a single Lambda process or by two different processes running on two different instances. If a process is modifying or accessing data and it needs to ensure conceptual consistency, aggregate it into a single function (and ideally a single request) instead of splitting it into multiple functions.

Data consistency is much easier to achieve with a single process than with multiple processes, even if they run the same code. Martin Fowler is often misquoted online for his apparent First Law of Distributed Computing ('Don't'), but the actual law he wrote about in *The Patterns of Enterprise Architecture*[2] is 'Don't distribute objects'. (For any domain-driven-design fans out there, this should really be 'Don't distribute aggregates'.) Having two different machines work on the same conceptual entity at the same time requires locking, transactions and conflict resolution. When a single instance owns a conceptual data entity and doesn't need to coordinate with other instances running on different machines, all these problems are easily avoided.

If two pieces of data need to be consistent with each other, make sure they are processed by a single instance of a single function. In the extreme case, limiting allowed concurrency to 1 ensures that only a single instance of a Lambda function ever runs, which can help avoid locking and conflict problems, but severely limits the total throughput of a process. Handling a lot of traffic often requires distribution, but the key to making this work is to avoid a network of tightly coupled systems. (The derogatory name for such architectures is a *distributed monolith*.) By aggregating code around data ownership, and letting different instances own different blocks of data, you can avoid tight coupling between instances and benefit from Lambda's auto-scaling capabilities.

Note that a common argument in favour of distributed systems over single-instance services is that more machines typically have better resilience than a monolith, but with Lambda this does not apply. The platform will handle failover and recovery automatically even if you set the concurrency limit to 1.

If you need to guarantee that a data entity will never be modified by more than one instance of a Lambda function at a time, you don't have to restrict Lambda to a single instance. Put a Kinesis Data Stream[3] between the requests and Lambda functions. Kinesis splits incoming events into shards (parallel processing units) and allows you to configure the partitioning data key. When Lambda reads events from a Kinesis stream, a single instance connects to a single shard and processes events in sequence. Although this doesn't make it possible to completely control routing between events and Lambda instances, it does make it possible to guarantee that there will be no more than one instance actively processing events for a specific key.

For example, at MindMup we use this trick to allow users to concurrently edit files. We use the file identifier as the partitioning key for Kinesis shards. Regardless of how many users send concurrent requests, all

[2]https://amzn.to/2IbWr5R
[3]https://aws.amazon.com/kinesis/data-streams

events for a single file will always end up in the same shard (events for other files may go to different shards). Because only one Lambda instance reads from a single shard, it can apply changes to an external file without having to worry about locking or concurrent modifications. We can control the total throughput of the system easily by configuring the number of shards.

If you need to guarantee a particular order of processing messages, but do not care about limiting overall parallelisation, you can set up a SQS FIFO (First-in-first-out) Queue and connect it to a Lambda function. When Lambda pulls messages with associated group identifiers from SQS, it will send only one batch per group identifier in parallel. It will then wait for an instance to successfully process that batch before pulling more messages from the same group. For more information, check out Using with Amazon SQS[4] page from the AWS Lambda Developer Guide.

Aggregate code that needs to be consistent

The second important technical constraint of the Lambda platform is that different functions don't deploy atomically. CloudFormation makes updates atomic in the sense that it will either completely succeed or completely roll back all the resources in a template, but it does not update all the Lambda functions at the exact same millisecond. It's best to design the code assuming that there will be a short period of time, even if it's a few milliseconds, where different functions may run with different versions of application code (or even that there will be two different versions of the same function running in parallel). As a consequence, if two pieces of code need to be fully consistent with each other at all times, put them in the same function. Code consistency is much easier to achieve with a single function than with multiple functions.

If several Lambda functions share data through an external repository, such as an S3 bucket or an SNS topic, consider adding a format version to the data when it leaves the Lambda function. For example, add a format version to the file metadata when saving a file to S3, or put the format version into message attributes when sending a message to an SNS topic. Format versions make it possible to reduce the need for strong code consistency across different functions. Data consumers can know what version of code saved or sent a particular piece of information, so they can decide to upgrade it, ignore some fields, or fall back to some alternative processing method for older events. This is a great trick for dealing with potential short inconsistencies between active versions in a large application.

Divide code around security boundaries

The third important technical constraint is that IAM security roles apply to whole functions. Different functions can have different security policies, but different parts of a function always run under the same privileges. If you need to reduce or increase the security privileges for some part of a process, it's better to extract that part into a separate Lambda function with a separate IAM role. Technically, you could use the AWS Security Token Service to change the security context inside a Lambda function, but doing that will be significantly more complicated than extracting a new function.

Smaller, more focused functions are less risky from a security perspective than a single bigger function that performs many tasks. When a Lambda function handles multiple types of request, it will need to have a

---

[4]https://docs.aws.amazon.com/lambda/latest/dg/with-sqs.html

sum of all the required security privileges. Because it is difficult to audit and tightly evaluate a complex set of tasks, aggregated services usually get full access rights on back-end resources. For example, a typical application server gets full read-write access to a user database. A single security hole in a third-party dependency of a monolith can let attackers steal a lot of data. When each task runs as an individual Lambda function, it's much easier to give it the minimum required access level. Breaking code down into smaller parts also makes it easier to audit and reduce security levels as a system evolves.

When deciding whether two pieces of code should stay together, consider whether they need the same access levels to other resources. If one function needs to modify some security-sensitive user data, and another function just needs to read that information, you can improve overall security by isolating the code into two different functions and giving the functions different IAM roles.

Divide code around CPU and memory needs

The fourth important constraint is financial instead of technical. Because Lambda charges for memory allocation multiplied by CPU time, bundling tasks with different memory needs can be unnecessarily expensive.

For example, at MindMup we run exporters for various formats. The PDF and SVG exporters share about 99% of the code. The PDF actually first produces an SVG image then runs an external tool to convert it to PDF. The external tool requires a lot of memory. The SVG exporter itself just works with a text file stream and needs very little memory. Putting both exporters into the same Lambda function would require us to pay for the memory needs of the PDF process when users export SVG files. Separating them allows us to reduce the allowed memory for the SVG function and pay significantly less.

People often bundle related code together just because the process is the same. When two different usages of the same piece of code have different CPU or memory needs, isolating those usages into two different functions can save a lot of money. Think about jobs (use cases) when deciding on Lambda granularity, not code units (functions).

Divide tasks around timing restrictions

A single Lambda invocation is limited to 15 minutes. For tasks that take longer, Lambda may not be the appropriate solution, or you may be able to work around the limit by splitting a task into several steps and potentially parallelising the work.

For example, I worked on an application to process documents uploaded by users. Processing each page took about 30 seconds, so Lambda functions could easily deal with relatively short documents, but users could upload documents with hundreds of pages. Instead of trying to do everything in a single task, we broke it down into three functions. The first would just split the uploaded document into pages and upload individual pages to another S3 bucket. It could easily process hundreds of pages in a few minutes. The second function would trigger when a page was uploaded to S3, and always process a single page. We could run hundreds of these functions in parallel. The third function would combine the results when the conversion process completed. Dividing the task into three functions like that made it possible to run everything in Lambda, but it also produced much faster results for users.

Dividing a job into smaller tasks due to timing restrictions typically requires an additional process to coordinate the execution of subtasks, periodically check for results and report on overall errors or success. One option for such an umbrella process is to move it to a client device, similar to the solution in Chapter 11. Another option is to implement the coordination inside AWS, but doing it as a Lambda function may not be the best idea, because the controller would still be restricted by the 15 minutes time limit. Instead, consider using AWS Step Functions[5]. Step functions are a mechanism for automating workflows with AWS resources, taking up to a year. You can configure parts of the workflow to invoke Lambda functions, pause or loop, and pass work between Lambda and other AWS services.

For tasks that cannot be parallelised, consider using AWS Fargate[6]. Fargate is a task management system for the Amazon Elastic Container Service with similar billing to Lambda functions. It will start and scale containers automatically based on demand, and charge you only for actual usage. There is no specific duration limit for Fargate tasks, so a single job can run for as long as it needs.

Fargate tasks start significantly more slowly than Lambda functions, but if the expected duration for a task is longer than 15 minutes, a few dozen seconds of warm-up time won't really make a noticeable difference. Instead of function source code, you'll need a Docker container image to deploy tasks to Fargate, but on the other hand that approach is a lot more flexible for packaging operating system utilities and third-party software. A single task can use up to 10 GB for the container storage, making Fargate a good option for situations where the 250 MB size limit for a function is too restrictive.

Sharing behaviour

As you start breaking down an application into Lambda functions, some of those functions will need to share behaviour. There are currently three options for that with Lambda functions:

- Common libraries
- Lambda layers
- Invoking one function from another

These options differ primarily in four aspects:

- Latency to execute shared code
- Runtime or deployment-time consistency
- Sharing across programming language runtimes
- Deployment speed and complexity

Bundling shared libraries

The first option is to extract common code into a shared programming language library and bundle it with each function. This minimises the latency to execute shared code, since it's just a quick in-memory call.

---

[5]https://aws.amazon.com/step-functions/
[6]https://aws.amazon.com/fargate/

Bundling dependencies with a function makes deployment simpler, but provides only deployment-time consistency. If you deploy just one function after changing the common code, all other functions will still run with the previous version. Common dependencies increase the package size for each function, so this is a good choice for typical programming language libraries, but may not be the best option for bundling a 100 MB native binary for a function that needs to redeploy frequently.

Shared libraries do not have any specific impact on SAM templates. The sam build command automatically bundles dependencies for Java, Python, Node.js and Go. Just list the common library in the appropriate package manifest of each dependent function (for example inside the dependencies section of package.json for JavaScript code). By the time you read this, it's highly probable that SAM will have started supporting building packages for some other languages.

In order to share data files or native Linux binaries using common dependencies, you may need to create a fake dependency package for your programming language of choice.

Working with Lambda layers

The second option is to extract common code into a Lambda layer. Layers also provide deployment-time consistency, similar to bundled dependencies, but they deploy once instead of with each function.

Dependencies included using layers also minimise latency to invoke shared code, since they effectively work inside the same container or memory space as the client code. Layers are good both for programming language libraries and for shared Linux binaries, because they can be attached to various runtimes. Functions written in JavaScript and Python can use the same layer. They cannot use the same shared programming language library.

Layers count towards the total available space for a function, so you can't work around the 250 MB Lambda code package limit by attaching layers.

Invoking one function from another

The third option is to extract common code into a separate Lambda function, and then invoke it from several other Lambda functions. Similar to using a layer, this makes it faster to deploy dependent functions. Unlike layers, the common code does not compete with other things in the dependent functions for the same 250 MB, since dependent Lambda functions deploy into different containers. Deploying as a separate function complicates the CloudFormation stacks slightly more than deploying layers. The dependent functions will need an IAM policy that allows them to talk to the common code.

The downside of invoking a different function is that the call latency is higher than with shared libraries or layers. Instead of simple memory access, invoking a Lambda function introduces network latency and a risk of network failure between the caller and the dependency. The benefit is that this is a runtime dependency. If five functions invoke the same common Lambda function and you deploy a new version of the common code, there's no need to redeploy the dependent functions as well.

Deploying a common function also makes it possible to share behaviour across programming languages. A Lambda function written in Python can easily call a Lambda function written in JavaScript, since they will use the Lambda protocol to communicate.

In Chapter 9 I explained the difference between synchronous and asynchronous Lambda events. When one Lambda function calls another, the caller can choose if they want to wait for the result (synchronous invocation) or just call the next function and ignore the outcome (asynchronous invocation). As a general rule of thumb, try structuring calls between functions to use the asynchronous method if you can. This will make the application cheaper (because the first Lambda function does not need to wait for the other), but it will also make it much easier to maintain and evolve the code. Chains of calls are much easier to maintain than loops, because dependencies always go in a single direction. Loops cause circular dependencies and tight coupling between the code of two functions.

For asynchronous function calls, I prefer to put a message queue between Lambda functions instead of directly invoking one from another. This forces me to think about the process through application events instead of remote procedure calls.

Consider the typical user registration scenario, split into two with two Lambda functions to reduce security risks. The first function writes new user information to a database. The second sends a welcome email without requiring database access. Thinking with remote procedure calls, the first function can invoke another and send a request similar to 'send welcome email to this address'. Designing with application events, the first function can save the new user record and then just publish an event similar to 'this user just registered; do whatever you need'. The second function can listen to user registration events and send the appropriate email.

In terms of source code, the difference between the two options is minimal. But in terms of future extensibility, it is huge. Later on, we might want to add another activity after users register, for example scheduling an introductory phone call. In the design with remote procedure calls we'd have to modify, retest and redeploy the first function to change the process. In the design with events, we just need to add another listener to the message queue. If we wanted to stop sending welcome emails later, we could just remove the listener for that specific function, without modifying or redeploying the function that writes user information to a database.

Sharing configuration

Related functions often need to share configuration, such as names of AWS resources or access keys to external services. In this book, we kept all the functions in a single SAM template and configured them using environment variables. Using a single template makes it easy to ensure that everything is configured consistently. This is great for simple examples, but only works if an entire application fits into a single SAM template. There are several reasons why a single template might not be the best option.

A single CloudFormation stack can only create 200 resources[7]. With SAM, that number is actually even lower, because SAM works as a CloudFormation transformation, so each `AWS::Serverless::Function` block translates into several resources. An application requiring more than 200 resources will need more than one template.

---

[7]https://docs.aws.amazon.com/AWSCloudFormation/latest/UserGuide/cloudformation-limits.html

First of all, large YAML files get difficult to maintain and are difficult to read. If you wouldn't create a single source code file with 200 variables, don't create a single CloudFormation template with 200 resources just because you can. In the same way as you'd split a large piece of code into smaller, more focused source code files, think about breaking up CloudFormation templates so that they are easy to understand and manage.

Larger organisations often have teams working on individual parts of an application, each with their own SAM templates or even groups of templates. For existing applications, parts might already be using some other deployment tools, so sometimes it's necessary to share configuration outside CloudFormation or to import it from a different resource.

If a single template is not enough, there are three main options for sharing configuration:

- Nested stacks
- Stack exports
- A parameter store

One of the 200 available resources in a stack can actually be a separate CloudFormation template describing an embedded application called, more technically, a *nested stack*. To use a nested stack, create a resource with the type `AWS::CloudFormation::Stack` and then point to a local SAM or CloudFormation template file using the `TemplateURL` property. You can then set the parameters of a nested stack or read out its outputs and use them to configure other nested stacks.

In order to configure applications consisting of several CloudFormation stacks, I usually create a separate template file just for configuration. This corresponds to the main entry file in a program. This template (usually `main.yaml`) contains the global application parameters, and it is just responsible for configuring modules as nested stacks. We used something very similar in Chapter 10, when importing an application from the Serverless Application Repository. Nested stacks allow you to do the same thing, just importing from a local file.

The benefit of maintaining configuration with parent and nested stacks is that it is very simple. The downside is that updating configuration requires redeploying the stack. A constraint of this approach is that all the modules need to be deployed together so that a parent stack can configure them all at once.

If you need to share configuration across modules that must be deployed separately, for example if they are created by different teams but everything is still managed by CloudFormation, consider exporting outputs from a stack. Include an `Export` field with an output of a stack, and CloudFormation will publish the value of that output in a registry where other CloudFormation templates can access it. In related stacks, use the `!ImportValue` function to read a property from the public registry. Similarly to nested stacks, updating exported and imported values also requires redeployment. For more information on this option, see the *Exporting Stack Output Values*[8] documentation page.

If you want to manage parts of an application using CloudFormation and parts using other tools, then the best option for sharing configuration is to use a parameter store. There are several AWS products for managing parameters, including the AWS Secrets Manager[9] and AWS Systems Manager Parameter Store[10].

AWS Secrets Manager and AWS Systems Manager Parameter Store are similar in many aspects. For example, you can read values from both in CloudFormation (using a feature called *dynamic references*[11] or using

---

[8]https://docs.aws.amazon.com/AWSCloudFormation/latest/UserGuide/using-cfn-stack-exports.html
[9]https://aws.amazon.com/secrets-manager
[10]https://docs.aws.amazon.com/systems-manager/latest/userguide/systems-manager-parameter-store.html
[11]https://docs.aws.amazon.com/AWSCloudFormation/latest/UserGuide/dynamic-references.html

the AWS SDK). This gives you the choice between applying configuration during deployment or reading the parameter values during Lambda function execution, which will increase the overhead and the price of individual functions but allow you to change the configuration without redeployment. As the name suggests, the Secrets Manager is intended for credentials such as passwords and access keys, and stores them securely. However, you can also require encrypted storage with the Systems Manager Parameter store.

There are two big differences between the tools. The Secrets Manager has some advanced features specific to storing access credentials, such as specifying a key rotation period and generating random values. It also costs significantly more. The Secrets Manager charges $0.40 for storing a single secret each month, and $0.05 for each 10,000 API calls. Using the Systems Manager Parameter store is effectively free for standard parameters.

Interesting experiments

- Change the thumbnail conversion application to use the AWS Systems Manager Parameter Store to configure the thumbnail width, allowed upload size and supported file types. Define hierarchies of settings for development, testing and production, and provide the environment as a parameter to CloudFormation during deployment.
- Split the thumbnail conversion application SAM template into several nested stacks. Use one stack to deploy the ImageMagick layer and the conversion function, and another stack to set up the web API. Use template outputs and parameters to configure resources. Create a main stack file that just connects the modules together.

Where next?

Check the website of this book at https://runningserverless.com for more information on related tools and topics. On the website, you can also get the source code from the book and check for any updates to the content.

Index

Lightning Source UK Ltd.
Milton Keynes UK
UKHW051136070721
386759UK00003B/28